Historic Tales of WINDHAM

Historic Tales of WINDHAM

DEREK SAFFIE

Forewords by Al Letizio Jr. & Rick Holmes

THE History PRESS

Published by The History Press
Charleston, SC
www.historypress.net

First published 2016

Manufactured in the United States

ISBN 978.1.46713.564.1

Library of Congress Control Number: 2016930874

Notice: The information in this book is true and complete to the best of our knowledge. It is offered without guarantee on the part of the author or The History Press. The author and The History Press disclaim all liability in connection with the use of this book.

To my great-grandfather Erich Obst, who returned home after serving in World War I and discovered for himself the everlasting allure of Cobbett's Pond.

CONTENTS

FOREWORD

We've been "Windham" for the better part of three hundred years. As of 2016, my family has been here for about forty of those years, so I am honored to have been asked by Derek Saffie to write the foreword for his *Historic Tales of Windham*.

In 1883, 164 years after its modern settlement, and 133 years ago, the first memorial of the "past and present" of Windham was penned by Leonard Allison Morrison, who opened his book with the words, "To the People of Windham N.H., and to those who derive descent from the Scotch settlers there, beneath whatever skies their homes might be, this memorial of the past and present is dedicated with sentiments of high regard." Back in 1883, Morrison listed 250 families by name. Today, Windham is the home to more than 5,000 families.

Ninety-two years after Morrison's book in 1975, the Windham Historic Committee asked, "What is Windham?" and after three hours of deliberation, dubbed it a "rural oasis," naming its newly published update of Windham's history by the same name. *Rural Oasis* is an important and well-written follow-up to Morrison's nineteenth-century work.

Many regard Windham's history as encompassing the last three hundred years of modern civilization. Recently, Derek Saffie and I visited Windham's historic "Indian Rock," our oldest known archaeological artifact, dating back thousands of years. I was amazed at how Derek brought this artifact to life for me and others by telling stories of the past and how this spot was so significant in its time. How many of our young people know about this and other important parts of our town's history? I would bet that most don't. Derek takes people, places and events that lie silently nestled in our past and brings them to life through stories and chronicles of our past. Humanizing these people, places and events makes them real for today's Windham residents and, building on the foundation created in earlier works, creates a fascinating connection from our past to our future.

The blending of old New England values and traditions, the fingerprints left on our town by generations of the past in historic places, is a treasure to be celebrated. It's one of the things that makes Windham so special. The symbols on our town crest—the castle towers, the water, the trees—all have meaning in our history and tell a story of who we are. My wife, Patti, and I were proud to commission in 2014 Windham's first flag, featuring our town crest prominently, and as of this writing, it is the only such flag in existence. We rely on storytellers to keep our history and those traditions preserved for the benefit of future generations.

Derek Saffie, a brilliant and thoughtful young mind of today, presents a fresh and modern interpretation of the history of our beloved home, Windham. He will now go down as the latest teller of our rich history, an embodiment of the spirit of Charles Knight, who, in 1883, said to Windham's future inhabitants: "History has a great office, to make the past intelligent to the present, for the guidance of the future."

Al Letizio Jr.
Chairman
Windham Board of Selectmen 2016

FOREWORD

I feel sure that Sir Charles Wyndham (1710–1763), Earl of Egremont, Baron Cockermouth, Baronet of Orchard Wyndham and Lord Lieutenant of Cumberland and Sussex, would be very proud of how the town named after him has turned out. The Wyndham family motto was, in fact, their war cry, "Au bon droit," which told the world they were fighting "with good reason." Perhaps that would also be a good motto for the town of Windham. Since our earliest days, the citizens of Windham have sent their children, husbands, sons and daughters to fight in a dozen wars, beginning with the French and Indian War and the Revolutionary War in the eighteenth century and on through the Civil War, the two world wars, Korea, Vietnam and the current conflicts in the Middle East. With each war, we proudly answered our country's call and fought "with good reason."

The town that is now Windham was settled in 1719 by a pioneer band of sixteen families led by the Reverend James MacGregor from Aghadowey in Northern Ireland. The land they were granted was originally called Nutfield and now makes up the towns of Derry, Londonderry and Windham, as well as parts of Hudson, Manchester and Salem. In 1722, Nutfield was given a charter by the royal governor and renamed Londonderry. On February 23, 1742, the southeastern portion of Londonderry was incorporated as the town of Windham.

The original Scotch-Irish Windham pioneers left the restrictions of the Old World to seek freedom in the wilderness of the New World, leaving Northern Ireland because of long years of persecution. In his last sermon in Ireland, Pastor MacGregor said they were going to America to seek religious, cultural, political and economic freedom. They were willing to leave the certainties of their Irish hearths and homes for the uncertainty of a wilderness settlement where, at night, they would hear the howls of wolves and live in fear of Indian attacks. Still, they would give up all they knew in Ireland in the pursuit of freedom for themselves and their progeny. One of the first things they did upon arrival was build a church so they could worship their God in their own way, a school so their children could read their Bibles and improve their lives economically and a meetinghouse so they could assemble to elect their own leaders and vote on taxing themselves for the common weal. All these civil and religious privileges had been denied to them under the oppressive rule of the British government in Ireland.

For nearly three centuries, the citizens of this town have worked to make Windham into a community, a warm, welcoming place with good neighbors that has a vision for the future and an appreciation of the past. Windham has seen itself change from a tiny frontier outpost in the middle of an endless forest into a town with an agriculture-based economy where there were truly more cows than people, the land was crisscrossed by miles and miles of stone walls and nearly 90 percent of the land was treeless pastures and fields. By the start of the twentieth century, farming in Windham had nearly died out, and much of the cleared land had been reclaimed by brush and trees.

Windham remained a small rural town for most of its history with its population very stable. In 1940, the town was home to only 630 people, about the same population as it had in 1790. Things soon changed, however. In 1963, Interstate 93 cut through the town, and immediately our population numbers began to rise. The town quickly became a desirable place to move to for those living in the crowded urban areas of the Bay State. Here in Windham were good schools, clean air and little crime. Another of the town's drawing cards was that now, because of the new highway, Windham was an easy commute to employment in the cities of Massachusetts.

For the rest of the twentieth century, the town's population doubled with the passing of every decade. Currently, Windham's population is nearly fourteen thousand, which is more than ten times what it was in 1960. Within the span of just two generations, Windham had changed from being known as a rural oasis to being considered on the fringe of the East Coast megalopolis that extends five hundred miles from the northern suburbs of Boston to northern Virginia. Demographically, most of today's town's residents are newcomers. They are not members of the old families who grew up knowing the stories and ways of their Windham ancestors. This book will serve to educate the newer residents about the history and traditions of their adopted hometown that they have quickly learned to love.

I suppose I am of the last generation to remember those times before television, when storytellers were the most popular form of local entertainment. So many, many times I remember sitting with my father in a neighbor's kitchen listening to the ancient ones tell stories of events that happened when the twentieth century was still young. These masters of the spoken words would also proudly tell about how, when they were boys, they met Civil War veterans and heard them tell their stories. I would listen with high interest to these secondhand tales of daring during the Battle of Gettysburg or the excitement of seeing old Abe Lincoln while they marched by him during a military review.

These stories passed down through the generations are the warp and woof of the fabric of the historical life of Windham. Through these stories, we can realize the hopes and aspirations of the founders of the town and better understand why Windham developed in the way it did. By studying the town's history, we learn what actions and policies were the most successful and which should be avoided. Through the stories in this book, we can once again put the spotlight on the many amazing personalities who strode and strutted across the stage of Windham's history. So many of these historical personages chronicled in this book can serve as excellent role models for our leaders, citizens and young people.

One importance of a book like this is to capture and retell the stories before the memories fade. How many times have you, I, we been told a story and, within a relatively short time, nearly forgotten it? With the passing of each of our old residents, a whole library of the town's stories is buried with him or her. A story or anecdote that is not written down can live only as long as it is remembered. The twice-told tales published in this book grant that story immortality. Well done, Windham. These stories, your stories, will now live forever.

Rick Holmes
Nutfield Historian

1

A LOOK AT WINDHAM

In order to fully appreciate the many stories of Windham's past, it is necessary to have a basic understanding of the historical layout of the town. The first detailed map of Windham was published in 1857 and recorded many of the local landowners and major geographical features. Another extensive map would not be completed until 1880, when a map of Rockingham County was compiled by Leonard A. Morrison for his history of Windham that was published three years later. This map contained the names of many Windham residents and geographical features, as well as several of the historical sites in town.

Historical names of local places are also evident on antique maps. For example, the small body of water on the eastern side of the map, labelled Hittitty Pond, has since been renamed Shadow Lake. Policy Pond, located just below Hittitty Pond, became known as Canobie Lake just a decade after the map was published. Maps, such as Morrison's, also present historians with mysteries. On his map of Windham, Morrison labelled a large tract of land the Gold Region. Bounded by roadways on three sides and a stream on the other, the area contains some of the highest points of elevation in Windham. Curiously, Morrison never makes any other reference to the region in his book. It is likely Morrison copied the name from the 1857 map without knowing exactly what was meant by the cartographers who originally gave the region the moniker. To this day, no one has been able to successfully solve the mystery of Windham's Gold Region.

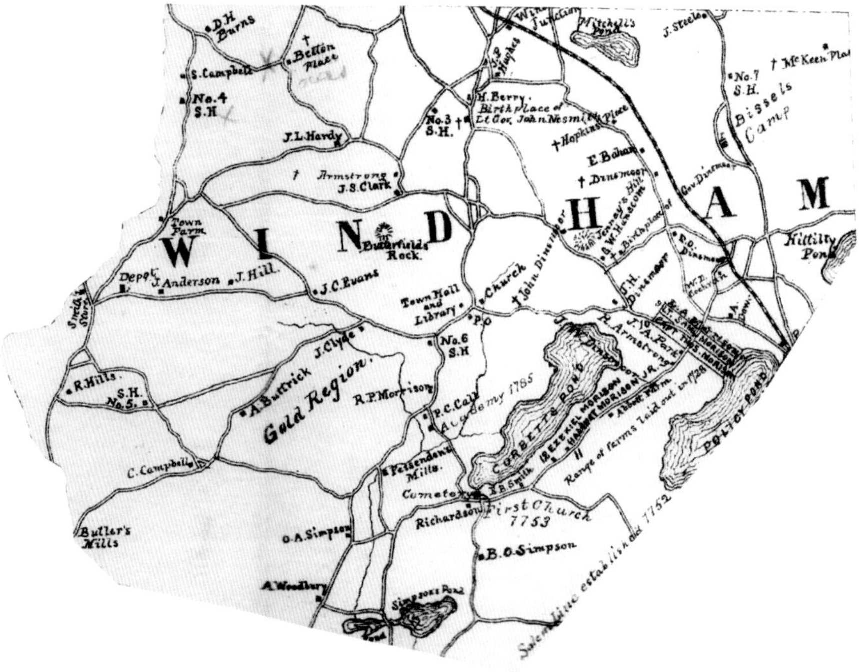

An 1880 map of Windham with several sites of historical significance marked. *From* History of Windham in New Hampshire (Rockingham County), 1719–1883.

The roads are another prominent feature of Morrison's map. Mentally navigating the system of roads provides an insightful look at the daily lives of Windham residents over one century ago. You can retrace the path many of Windham's most well-known citizens traversed to reach the town hall or attend the Sunday service at the Presbyterian church. There are even some roads that still exist today, in almost the same location they were over one hundred years ago. Range Road is one such road. Located on the eastern side of Cobbett's Pond, the road runs the entire length of the pond and beyond. Some of the earliest settlers of Windham lived in the vicinity of what is now known as Range Road. The roads are just one of a wealth of features offered on the earliest detailed maps of Windham. Featured in this introductory chapter, the 1880 map is an interesting look back into Victorian era Windham.

2

THE FOUNDING OF WINDHAM

The Native Americans

The earliest inhabitants of Windham were Native Americans belonging to the Penacook tribe, commonly known as the Pawtuckets. While it is unknown how early the area was inhabited, it was certainly centuries before the first Europeans arrived. The earliest recorded interaction between Europeans and the local Pawtuckets occurred around 1653, when missionaries—namely, John Eliot—preached at the Pawtucket Falls in Lowell, Massachusetts. However, the importance of Pawtucket Falls in Windham's Native American history reaches far beyond interactions with Christian missionaries. The falls, located a convenient twelve miles from Windham, were a valuable source of fish. It is recorded that up until 1818, when the water from the falls was redirected for Lowell's burgeoning factories, the roar of the falls and rushing waters below could easily be heard in Windham.

The Pawtucket in Windham certainly camped along the shores of Cobbett's Pond and Canobie Lake, as numerous arrowheads and Native American artifacts have been found over the last century at both locations. Such artifacts include the stone tools handcrafted by tribesmen for various uses, such as skinning animals. Arguably, the most prominent of the Pawtucket relics in town is Indian Rock. Located just a short distance from the north shore of Cobbett's Pond, the large boulder stands around five feet high and is several feet wide. It is surrounded by several slightly smaller boulders, none of which bears any evidence of use by the Pawtucket tribe.

On the top are several circular holes a few inches deep and several inches in diameter that were, at one time, used by the Native Americans for pounding corn and other grains. Those interested in the early history of Windham can still visit this rock, which is marked by a plaque placed on the front of the boulder in 1933. Windham is also home to another unusual Native American site, aptly named Deer Ledge; the Pawtuckets once chased a deer over the ledge, into the waters of Rock Pond below.

In the mid-seventeenth century, the tribe was headed by its last great chief, Passaconnaway. In the 1660s, Passaconnaway, at the advanced age of somewhere between 90 and 110 years old, believed he did not have many years of life left. A feast and dance were held, at which he warned his people to be peaceful with the Europeans, as this would be the only way to ensure the survival of the tribe. The tribe heeded his warning and had little contact with the Europeans of southern New Hampshire. The Pawtuckets did not remain in Windham long after Passaconnaway's death around 1679. They relocated the headquarters of the tribe to Concord, New Hampshire, several years following the chief's passing. However, for the next fifty years, the Pawtucket tribe continued to travel to Pawtucket Falls, undoubtedly traveling through the primitive settlement at Nutfield, which encompassed the modern towns of Londonderry, Derry and Windham and, to a lesser extent, portions of Hudson, Manchester and Salem.

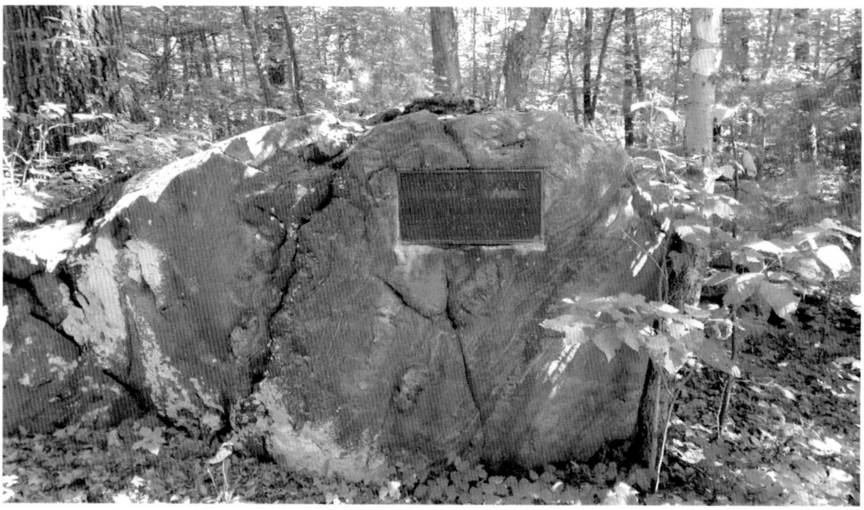

The front of Indian Rock showing a plaque placed on the boulder in 1933. *Author's collection.*

One of the only recorded interactions between the Pawtuckets and the settlers of Nutfield occurred in a tragic way in 1721. Just a couple years after the Scotch-Irish arrived in Nutfield, a party of men was traveling from Haverhill, Massachusetts, to the home of Daniel Gregg. On the way, the men spotted a small site near some rocks that would serve as an ideal location to stop and rest before continuing to their destination. After lighting a fire and eating their dinner, they continued on. In time, they realized they had forgotten something at the camp, though there is no record that indicates exactly what was left at their makeshift campsite. A young boy who was traveling with the group was sent back to retrieve it, but he would never again see his fellow travelers. When the boy had not returned to the group within a reasonable time, the men went back to the location they had camped and found his body. The boy had been killed by a member of the Pawtucket tribe on the banks of Golden Brook near the home of James Noyes. The boy's body was buried on the banks of the brook with no marker to denote the place of the first death and burial in Windham.

Eventually, the tribe completely removed to Canada, leaving little trace of their existence in Windham. Only a few of the earliest settlers were aware of their presence. Leonard A. Morrison concluded his writing on the Native Americans in town with a poem, which is as fitting in his work as it is in this one:

I will go to my tent and lie down in despair,
I will paint me with black and sever my hair;
I will sit on the shore when the hurricane blows,
And reveal to the God of the tempest my woes.
I will weep for a season, on bitterness fed,
For my kindred are gone to the mounds of the dead.

THE SCOTCH-IRISH ARRIVE IN NUTFIELD

The earliest settlers of Nutfield were driven to the New World by the unrest in seventeenth-century Ireland. Many of those who left Ireland for America in 1718 were survivors of the 1689 siege of Londonderry. The siege on the walled city began shortly after King James II of England was deposed by his daughter and son-in-law, William. James fled to France, hoping to gain support in order to try to gain control of Ireland and eventually take back the throne in England. With aid he received from the French, James's forces were able to capture Dublin, as well as the surrounding region. This forced many of the British supporters to flee to the north, with some going to the city of Londonderry. Those in the fortified city would prove to be the most formidable opponents James had ever, or would ever, face.

On April 20, 1689, James began his bombardment of the city; many lives were lost and countless buildings were destroyed by the resulting fires. James's forces also blockaded any routes by which the city might receive supplies, leaving the survivors of the first attacks without the food needed to survive more than a couple months. Still, the people of Londonderry steadfastly refused to surrender. A clergyman of the town, George Walker, would routinely give strong sermons that instilled in the listeners enough courage and strength to continue their fight even as conditions worsened. Horse meat became a highly desired commodity, and when the meat ran out, even the hides of horses were consumed. When all the edible parts of the town's horses, including the blood, had been consumed, the townspeople were forced to eat any remaining small animals, including dogs, rats, mice and cats.

Months passed, and the food supply had been diminished to just one pint of food per person. It was estimated that most individuals would be able to survive for only another two days with the supplies on hand. Despite the circumstances, those still alive refused to surrender. After 103 days under siege, the British finally managed to break through the blockades and bring much-needed supplies to Londonderry. With more strength than ever to fight to hold the city, Londonderry was held by British supporters until July 31, when the enemy finally withdrew, without much of a fight. Just under a year later, the armies of James were finally defeated by William, his successor.

The government of England felt that the heroic acts of the people of Londonderry were so important to the nation that all who fought in the siege were exempted from taxation. When a group of these people came to Nutfield seeking religious freedom, they were given the same tax-exempt status until the American Revolution. Along with these men came families and other members of their community, all led by Reverend James MacGregor. When the group reached America in 1718, some chose to settle in the Casco Bay area while others went to such towns as Andover and Dracut, Massachusetts. By April 13, 1719, a group of the immigrants had arrived in Haverhill, where they heard of an unsettled tract of land referred to as "Chestnut Country"; the name was derived from the abundance of chestnut trees in the area. Thus, the land was christened Nutfield by the first settlers.

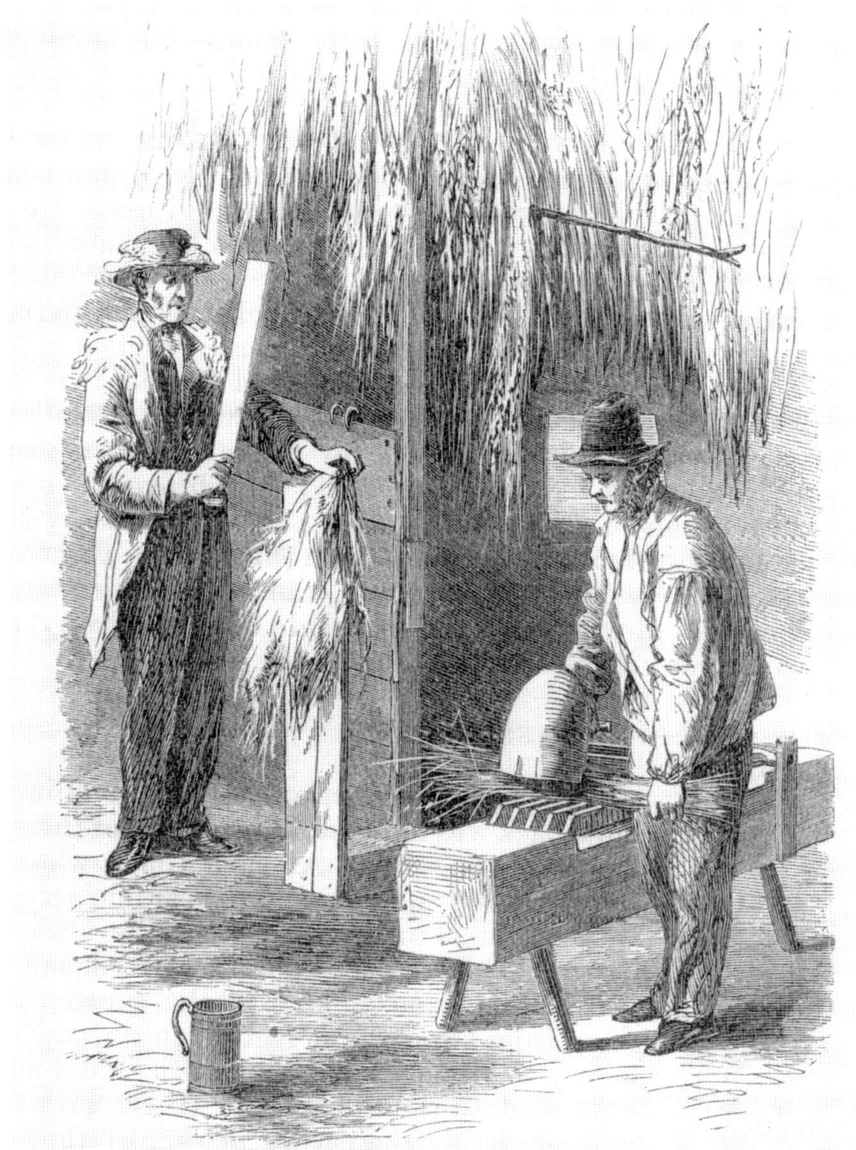

A nineteenth-century engraving depicting how early settlers would have processed their flax into linen. *From* History of Windham in New Hampshire (Rockingham County), 1719–1883.

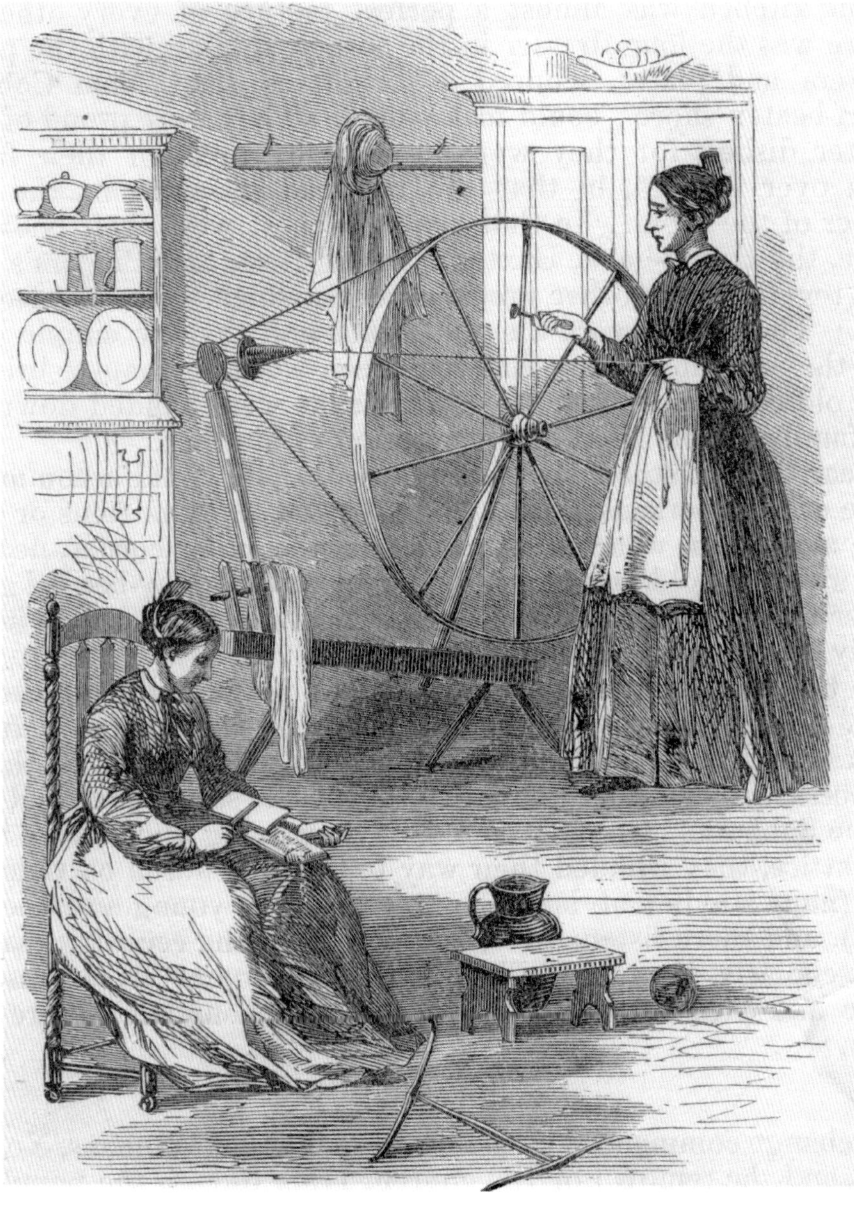

A nineteenth-century engraving depicting an early eighteenth-century home scene similar to what would have been found in the homes of early settlers. *From* History of Windham in New Hampshire (Rockingham County), 1719–1883.

Many of the men of the group left their families in order to make their way to Nutfield to see if it would be suitable for a small community. Finding promise in the land, they received a grant for twelve square miles from the royal governor of the Massachusetts Bay Colony. After building a few temporary huts, the men returned to Haverhill to bring their families and possessions back to Nutfield. The party stopped in Dracut allowing Reverend MacGregor to join them; the entire group arrived in Nutfield on April 22, 1719.

Although the community started small, it grew to include seventy families within the first five months. One month later, it had grown to around 105 families. The rapid growth of the settlement necessitated the incorporation of Nutfield as a town, but it would be almost three years before Londonderry was finally incorporated on June 21, 1722. The town continued to grow, and running a town of that size eventually became cumbersome. Such was at least part of the reason why Windham split from Londonderry and was incorporated on February 23, 1742, by Governor Benning Wentworth.

Reverend Thomas Cobbet

Thomas Cobbet was born in Newbury, England, in 1608 to a financially poor family. He studied at Oxford as a young man but decided to immigrate to America to alleviate his fear of being stricken with the plague. Cobbet arrived in America on June 26, 1637, and became a colleague of Reverend Samuel Whiting of Lynn, Massachusetts; even though Lynn had been settled just eight years before, the population had already grown enough to warrant the services of two ministers. He was known for being a very serious man who was both revered and feared by many who attended his services. On one occasion, it was recorded that a few of his neighbors, all women, were practicing some sort of witchery. Before they had finished, Reverend Cobbet was spotted walking toward them. The women stopped immediately, and one verbalized her disdain for Cobbet by yelling that "crooked-back Cobbet" was coming.

After only one year of service, Cobbet was granted two hundred acres of land in Lynn. In 1654, he was appointed as an overseer of Harvard College by the General Court of Massachusetts. He served as a minister in Lynn until 1656, when he became pastor of a church in Ipswich, Massachusetts. Cobbet was also an author and published several books on the subject of religion during his lifetime, one of which was well received by Cotton Mather. He became a prominent member of his community and was eventually able to secure the first grant for land in the area that became Windham. The land, surrounding the pond that would one day bear his name, was surveyed in October 1662 and approved by the General Court of Boston on May 27, 1663. The land composing Windham was under the control of Massachusetts until a separate government was established to form New Hampshire in 1680.

It is unknown if Cobbet ever visited his land in Windham, as there were no apparent improvements made on it, nor were there any European settlers on it before 1719. Cobbet did remain at his post in Ipswich until his death on November 5, 1685. His mourners consumed a barrel of wine and two barrels of cider at his funeral; spice and ginger were added to the cider as the day was quite cold. He was survived by his wife, Elizabeth, and four children: Samuel, John, Thomas and Elizabeth. His wife passed away one year later.

3

THE SHIPWRECK OF THE *CATHERINE*

The flow of immigrants to Nutfield did not stop after the group led by James McGregor arrived in 1719. Emigrants looking to join their family and friends or simply looking to start life anew in America continued to leave Ireland for decades following the original settlement of Nutfield. One of those groups left for America on the ship *Catherine* in 1737. On June 4 of that year, the ship departed from Rush, a small seacoast town in Dublin, Ireland, with 202 passengers aboard. The ship carried solely the belongings of the passengers, which included enough gold and silver for the ship to be considered the richest vessel to have ever departed from Ireland at the time.

The 110-ton snow, a ship similar to a brig, left port with Commander Robert Walker at the helm and Adam McNeal and David Thompson as freighters, their job being to load the cargo onto the ship. Expecting to arrive in Boston, Massachusetts, in just over two weeks, the passengers had a relatively mundane and easy passage until thirteen days into their trip, when they neared Nova Scotia. On that day, the weather made a turn for the worse when the wind began blowing with a frightening strength and large waves slammed against the ship. The ship's tiller, used to steer the rudder, was broken in two, and the ship was eventually grounded on a large sandbar about a mile from the nearest shore. However, the power of the seas proved to be great enough to free the *Catherine* from the sandbar, driving it straight to the shore.

Once the *Catherine* was finally run aground, the weather began to tear the ship apart. First went the main mast, which was carried away by the current.

Within minutes, the ship was broken into pieces, leaving the passengers at the whim of the raging storm. It is unclear if any of the passengers had perished prior to the ship's being driven ashore by the storm. All that is known is that ninety-eight people, almost half the ship's passengers, died in the torrential currents off the shore of Nova Scotia. Among those who were killed were two prominent Irish cloth merchants who had intended to manufacture diapers, fabric with a woven design that made it more absorbent, in America.

The rest of the passengers were forced to the shore by the waves, battered and bruised from the debris of the shipwreck. Some of their injuries were so severe that several more passengers died soon after they reached the shore. Waiting until daylight to venture farther onto the island, the group gathered on the side of a nearby hill where they erected a makeshift tent out of the main sail from the ship. Numerous featherbeds were also washed ashore with the sail, and these were used by the survivors to shelter themselves from the inclement weather on the island. When the weather became more hospitable, the group of survivors did their best to provide a proper burial for the bodies of the deceased that had washed ashore.

Although one of the ship's longboats did survive the storm, it was riddled with holes and, thus, required about two days' worth of work to be restored to usable condition. With tools scavenged from a carpenter's chest that had washed ashore, the men of the group did their best to repair the boat using pieces of broken boards and some canvas from the sail. A group of nine men, including the freighters, navigated the salvaged longboat about 110 miles to the town of Canso, Nova Scotia. They made good time, reaching the town in just three days.

After arriving in Canso, the group alerted the governor and several other men about the shipwreck and the remaining survivors. Acting with a sense of compassion, a schooner was readied, and a ship's captain was located to rescue the survivors. Leaving on the day after the men arrived in Canso, the schooner reached the rest of the survivors, some being very weak and requiring the care of a doctor, the next day. The schooner brought the survivors to a now unknown town where half of them eventually went by ship to Piscataqua. About half of this group then made their way to Nutfield.

Among the group on the ship were members of the Tufts family. A period newspaper account notes that a John Tufts perished in the shipwreck. However, some of the literature relating to the history of the Tufts family suggests another Tuft, a young boy also named John, might have survived the wreck and eventually come to live with a childless family in Nutfield. It is important to keep in mind that Tufts family historians have conflicting stories of John's life before he came to Windham. One conflicting account says he was born in Massachusetts; however, the true story of the early years of his life has likely been forever lost to history.

What is known is that he was born in 1723 and would have been only fourteen at the time of the shipwreck. He became a deacon and is recorded as having arrived in Windham sometime around 1745. In 1752, he purchased land from Jonathan Morrison on the east side of town. There he constructed a sawmill a few years later. He sold his land on June 30, 1774, seeking to move to Maine, where he lived until his death in 1802. Tufts became one of the founders of the city of Belfast.

Before leaving Windham, John Tufts invented an astronomical instrument to aid in navigation. His motivation is unknown, but it is likely he had wanted to prevent shipwrecks like the one that killed his parents. Ship navigation was still rather crude in the later half of the eighteenth century, and had his invention proved useful, it could have been a potentially valuable instrument to sea captains. Although there is no evidence that his instrument ever progressed beyond the development stage, New Hampshire governor Wentworth saw promise in the invention and invested ten dollars into its development in 1773.

4

THE GREAT MERINO SHEEP CRAZE

Before the discovery of gold in California and Alaska, Americans were caught up in a craze unlike any the nation has ever seen before or since. Up until the early nineteenth century, the export of Merino sheep from their native land of Spain was banned. The breed of sheep was desired throughout Europe and North America for its high-quality wool, which was known for its water-repellant qualities. At that time, almost every flock of Merino sheep was owned by either the Catholic Church or the Spanish royal family, with a few rare exceptions of flocks of the sheep being given as gifts to Spanish nobility. Merino sheep were so prized by Spain's ruling family that the penalty for taking even one sheep beyond the borders of the nation was death.

Much like the Chinese porcelain and silk of centuries ago, the government saw the sheep as an asset to their nation, which they were able to control. For centuries, Spain controlled the Merino sheep market with an iron fist. However, William Jarvis, the U.S. consul to Lisbon, Portugal, arrived in the nation at an opportune time, just as Napoleon Bonaparte was beginning to break Spain's monopoly on the sheep. Jarvis was successful in purchasing a flock of Merino sheep from the royal family. The exportation of the four thousand sheep he purchased would signal the crumbling of Spain's sheep empire. Thus, Jarvis was forced to smuggle the sheep out of Spain and onto the ship awaiting to bring him, and the flock, back to the United States. Since he was still on official duty from the U.S. government, Jarvis ensured his superiors were notified throughout the smuggling operation.

The sheep were brought back to Jarvis's farm in Weathersfield, Vermont. Eight sheep were gifted to Thomas Jefferson, as it was Jefferson who appointed Jarvis to his post, and several sheep were also given to then president James Madison. However, Jarvis did not want to keep the valuable sheep in the hands of the aristocratic class as they had been in Europe. Instead, he set out on a nationwide tour to publicize the Merino sheep. As farmers and entrepreneurs began to see the foundations of profitable businesses in the sheep market, Jarvis began to breed and sell flocks of the once rare sheep to anyone who was interested. He eventually branched out into selling Merino wool throughout Europe and America.

Jarvis owed a great deal of his success in the sheep business to fortunate timing with world politics, not only when he obtained the sheep but also when he began to sell the sheep. When blockades during the War of 1812 prevented British wool from reaching America, the demand for domestically produced wool soared. Americans were now able to purchase some of the finest-quality wool in the world. Farmers all over the eastern states, especially those of New England, clamored at Jarvis's door wanting to buy as many Merino sheep as they could raise.

There were undoubtedly at least a few farmers in Windham who could not resist the allure of the exotic sheep. One of these was David Gregg, whose pasture on a hill just happened to be the perfect grazing grounds for his newly acquired Merino sheep. So enamored of this new business, Gregg constructed a stone wall by hand to enclose about thirty-four acres of pastureland for his sheep. One can imagine the time spent as Gregg, and very likely some hired hands, toiled away day after day to build stone walls a couple feet high in a near perfect square that measured about 1,200 feet on each side. Gregg was not alone in constructing stone walls, as almost a quarter million miles of them were constructed across New England to serve as enclosed meadows for sheep.

While Gregg went about his new operation with determination and a strong work ethic, not everyone anxious to get into the sheep business was so honest. Although his surname has been lost to history, there is a record of a man by the name of Joseph, who, not wanting to construct time- and labor-intensive stone walls, decided to build a small pen out of large pine branches in the woods near his home. Next, he absconded with several sheep from his neighbor's pens, having in mind an unusual scheme to keep his stolen property undetected. As sheep were an important part of a farmer's livelihood, each animal was marked on the ear in a distinctive way to indicate the owner. To remedy this problem, Joseph cut off the ears of the sheep he

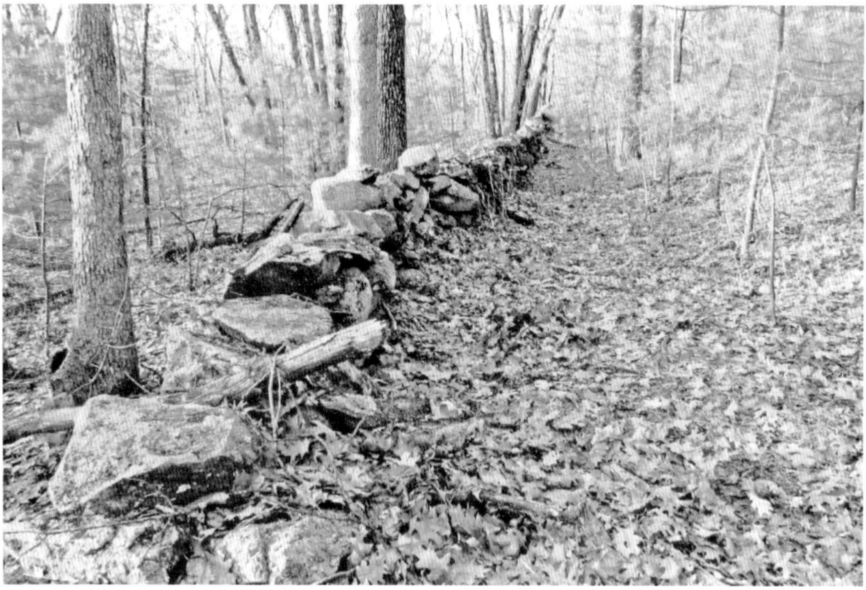

The wall of the sheep pen on the former pastureland of David Gregg. *Windham Historic District/Heritage Commission.*

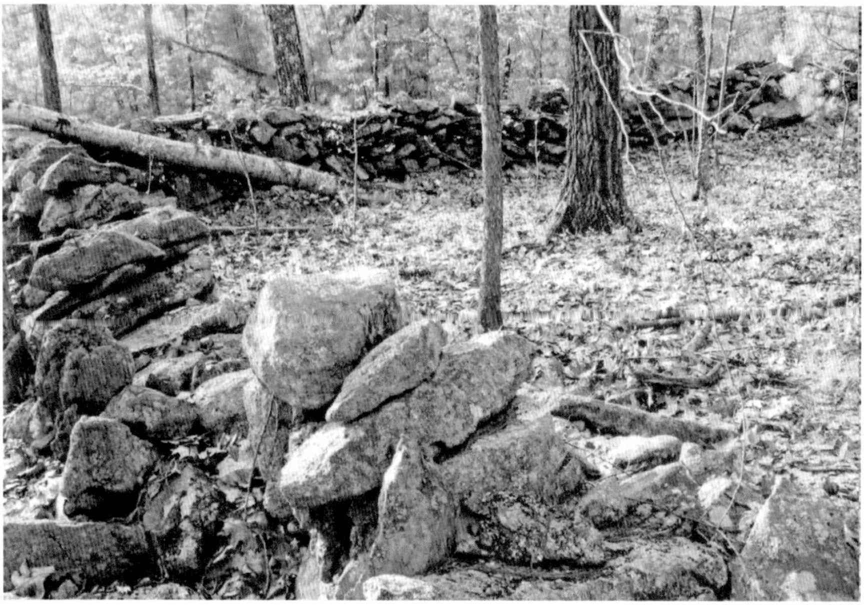

One of the corners of the Gregg sheep pen. *Windham Historic District/Heritage Commission.*

stole close enough to their heads so that it would be impossible to determine their rightful owner. Whether Joseph succeeded in his scheme might never be known, but it is certainly a telling story of what desperate measures a man will go to when he becomes obsessed with a financially lucrative craze.

As there were no woolen mills located in Windham at the time, the Merino wool produced in town was likely either sold to local woolen mills or merchants. Not only did the Merino wool reach the price of fifty-seven cents per pound during the craze, but the specific breed of sheep was also more productive than the other two breeds that were previously popular. Merino sheep were able to produce wool to a ratio of about 15 percent of its total body weight. The other breeds of sheep usually yielded wool equivalent to about 6 percent of body weight.

However, Windham farmers, such as David Gregg, were eventually forced out of the Merino sheep business due to changing economic conditions, including the introduction of tariffs. During the 1820s and 1830s, the U.S. government was continually changing tariff laws, sometimes favoring the domestic producers of wool and other times favoring imported wool. As Europe was also a large player in the Merino wool market, they proved to be cutthroat competition for the small-time farmers and larger merchants of the Northeast. Jarvis worked hard to save the market he had created, spending tens of thousands of dollars trying to convince legislators, and the public, to support measures to protect American wool producers.

However, Jarvis was unsuccessful, and the wool market continued to deteriorate. As a result, the pasture on the high hills of the Gregg family's farm fell out of use, and the land was sold to Asa Buttrick of Pelham, New Hampshire, just as the Merino sheep craze was winding down. While prior to the Industrial Revolution the typical Windham family might have kept a small flock of sheep for personal use, this tradition faded out along with the Merino sheep craze. With the advent of mills in Lowell and Lawrence, Massachusetts, woolen goods could be more easily mass produced. Purchasing manufactured woolen goods, or even wool itself, became easier and more affordable than raising sheep.

By 1840, the price of Merino wool had dropped to only twenty-five cents per pound. Although the farmers of Windham and southern New Hampshire were affected by the downturn of the wool market, the farmers of Vermont were hit especially hard. The relatively low cost of wide expanses of land in the new western territories made it much more affordable to compete with the farmers in the East. While those willing to make the arduous journey to the West were rewarded with competitive advantages in the wool market, some East Coast farmers were forced to slaughter their flocks rather than spending the money to feed them.

The downturn in the sheep market also came at a time when the new factory jobs being created in Lowell and Lawrence began to look more attractive to the younger generation of Windham than a life of farming. Most of the young men lured away from Windham by mill jobs were interested in the money they could make; many of them had helped to construct the dam and canals of Lowell and realized how lucrative that line of work could be. Almost all young boys over the age of fourteen left Windham for one of the mill cities, with some as young as twelve preferring millwork to work on the family farm. Not only was the pay better, but there were also many other benefits to working in the mills.

The millworkers were provided housing in recently built boardinghouses that were much more attractive to young boys than a room at the family homestead. Also, there were many young women working at the mills, and this arrangement proved to be quite enticing to teenage boys. There were certainly many more young ladies at the mills than in a small, rural town. In fact, many of the young men remained in Lowell for the rest of their lives, leaving Windham nearly void of an entire generation. This also contributed to a large decline in the population of Windham, a problem compounded even further when the older residents of Windham left town in order to join their children in Lowell or elsewhere in the country.

The trend of younger generations leaving Windham with the advent of new technology, such as that which led to the development of the railroad or that which spawned the Industrial Revolution, became unfortunately all too common in rural New Hampshire towns, where idyllic ponds and woods proved to be no match for the promise of new, exciting industries. Even more unfortunate for the agriculture industry in general, wool production was one of the largest sectors of New England's economy, and many farmers struggled to feed their families, with the luckier farmers simply moving into another line of business. As with the Dutch tulip craze, gold rushes and many other crazes and fads of the past, the story of the Merino sheep craze remains a testament to the disadvantages of risking it all when jumping on the bandwagon of the latest moneymaking scheme.

5

THE "RUSTIC BARD"

Windham range in flowery vest,
Was seen in robes of green,
While Cobbet's pond, from east to west,
Spread her bright waves between.
Cows lowing, cocks crowing,
While frogs on Cobbet's shore,
Lay croaking and mocking
The bull's tremendous roar.

The above is just one short excerpt from the work of Windham's Deacon Robert Dinsmoor, a renowned Scotch-Irish poet better known as the "Rustic Bard." Born in Windham on October 7, 1757, to one of the town's founding families, Dinsmoor had a childhood typical of that of many young boys during the period. As was common in colonial America, especially in a newly settled rural town, Dinsmoor was not afforded the luxury of an education until he was nine years old. His earliest experience with education came from an old British soldier who came to the Nutfield area following his service in the French and Indian War. The elderly soldier taught young Dinsmoor biblical scriptures, which he would memorize regardless of length. Even at a young age, he was able to appreciate the benefits of the education he was receiving and is recorded as having written to a friend that he hoped he would never stray from this religious background.

Dinsmoor's first experience with a formal education came several years later when he became a pupil of a man known as Master McKeen. Not only did McKeen instruct his pupils in the academic subjects of the day, but he also often took them squirrel hunting. If anyone can be credited with launching Dinsmoor's poetical career, it might be McKeen, as it was under the direction of this teacher that the young man was first exposed to academic writing, as well as English. Although Dinsmoor excelled in both the former and latter subjects, he lamented later on in life that he had not performed well in arithmetic because he was too busy with his involvement in an early love interest.

With the advent of the Revolutionary War, Dinsmoor joined the army at the age of eighteen. Although he served only three months, one of the highlights of his military career was serving at the Battle of Saratoga. Dinsmoor later served in the army again for several short periods of time. With military life behind him by the time he was twenty-five, Dinsmoor married Mary Park of Windham and settled down to spend the rest of his life farming the open fields on the east side of Cobbett's Pond, land that had belonged to his father. Serving as an elder in the Windham Presbyterian church for about fifty years, Dinsmoor certainly remained true to his faith and discharged his duties as a deacon with the utmost sincerity and devotion.

Dinsmoor had been a talented poet since relatively early in his life. It is during this period of his life that he adopted the nom de plume "Rustic Bard," which he signed to his earliest newspaper contributions. His work was usually marked by a distinctive Scotch-Irish dialect that had ties to his ancestral roots. This nod toward his ancestry reflected his love for the Scotch-Irish customs, language and culture. Several of his poems do make a direct reference to his heritage. However, many of his other works were written for various reasons.

One, according to John Greenleaf Whittier, was written to relate a priest's frustration as a dog "rattled and scraped" at the door while a sermon was being given. Whittier also noted that Dinsmoor wrote poems to "amuse his neighbors" and sometimes to ease tensions after a "domestic calamity." The bard also wrote about farm life and ordinary events, usually writing using the common man's dialect, describing things plainly and simply. A notable example of a poem based on his own life was written shortly after the death of his wife. An excerpt from the work is as follows:

No more may I the Spring Brook trace,
No more with sorrow view the place
Where Mary's wash-tub stood;
No more may wander there alone,

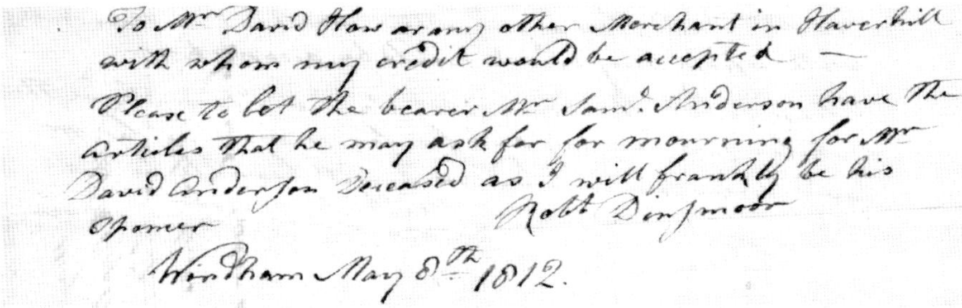

To Mr David How or any other Merchant in Haverhill
with whom my credit would be accepted —
Please to let the bearer Mr Saml. Anderson have the
articles that he may ask for for mourning for Mr
David Anderson deceased as I will frankly be his
Opomer
Robt Dinsmoor
Windham May 8th 1812.

The promissory note signed by Deacon Robert Dinsmoor allowing Samuel Anderson to obtain any articles required for the mourning of his father, David Anderson. *Author's collection.*

And lean upon the mossy stone
Where once she piled her wood.
'Twas there she bleached her linen cloth,
By yonder bass-wood tree;
From that sweet stream she made her broth,
Her pudding and her tea.
That stream, whose waters running,
O'er mossy root and stone,
Made ringing and singing,
Her voice could match alone

Reflecting on his late wife doing the family's laundry and retrieving water from a nearby stream for cooking, Dinsmoor wrote about the daily chores that represented some of his most cherished memories of his late wife, who passed away at the age of thirty-eight in 1799.

On December 31, 1801, Dinsmoor married Mary Anderson, the widow of Samuel Anderson of Londonderry. Marrying a father of twelve, Mary was forced to quickly adjust to the arduous task of being a stepmother to such a large family. Shortly after moving to the Dinsmoor homestead, she became a motherly figure not only to her own children, and eventually grandchildren, but also to the young children of the community, who affectionately gave her the nickname "Aunt Molly."

It was after his marriage to Mary Anderson that Dinsmoor began to take his poetry more seriously, publishing many works in local periodicals. In 1828, a collection of the Bard's poems were published in a small volume printed in Haverhill, Massachusetts. It was this publication that can be given much of the credit for cementing Dinsmoor in his place as one of history's preeminent Scotch-Irish poets. Unbeknownst to the original audience of

Dinsmoor's *Incidental Poems*, a relatively unknown poet by the name of John Greenleaf Whittier who contributed a single poem to the book would become one of the greatest poets in the history of the nation. Whittier and Dinsmoor became friends, but the two seldom interacted with each other.

In about 1816, Dinsmoor was the victim of a "paralytic shock" that nearly claimed his life. He also suffered from severe rheumatism later in his life, which at times made it impossible for him to stand completely erect. Nearing the end of his life, Dinsmoor is described by Whittier as:

> *chaffering in the market-place of my native village, swapping potatoes and onions and pumpkins, for tea, coffee, molasses, and, if the truth be told, New England rum…He still stood stoutly and sturdily in his thick shoes of cowhide, like one accustomed to tread independently the soil of his own acres,—his broad, honest face seamed by care and darkened by exposure to "all the airts that blow," and his white hair flowing patriarchal glory beneath his felt hat. A genial, jovial, large-hearted old man, simple as a child.*

The Rustic Bard died of pneumonia at the age of seventy-nine on March 16, 1836. His widow lived on to survive him by nearly two years, dying on January 19, 1838.

6

THE MYSTERIOUS DEATH OF REVEREND SIMON-FINLEY WILLIAMS

Everyone has heard some variation of this age-old mystery. Someone passes away only to "return" to their friends and family years later. From television series and movies to novels, this popular genre of mystery might sound more like science fiction than reality. However, such an occurrence is not reserved for the realm of fiction. It did happen in Windham.

Simon-Finley Williams was born in Princeton, New Jersey, on July 23, 1764, to parents Simon Williams and Maria Floyd Williams. The elder Simon Williams was born in Ireland in 1729 and at the age of sixteen became engaged to a young lady his age who was of a much higher social standing than himself. The young woman, Maria Floyd, was the daughter of Captain John Floyd, Esquire, who served under General Honeywood in the British army. Her parents did not see the sense in her marrying someone of a lower social standing and forbade the marriage to take place. Refusing to let such an obstacle stand in the way of their being together, Simon and Maria fled to England.

Fortunately for the young couple, King George II took an interest in them and paid for their schooling. As was common in the day, Simon furthered his education beyond what Maria, as a woman, would have been expected to complete. After Simon became a learned man, the couple was married on April 30, 1749, in London. The king then sent them to St. Thomas Island, where Simon spent several years teaching. Sometime around 1758, the family, which grew to include three children born to the couple in Jamaica, moved to Philadelphia, Pennsylvania, where Simon continued his profession as a teacher.

Wanting to further his education, Simon took up studies at the College of New Jersey, graduating in 1763. Having become interested in religion through the preaching of Reverend Gilbert Tennent, it is believed he may have wanted an American college education to ease his way into a position in the church. At the time he graduated, and for some time after, the Williams family resided in Fogg's Manor, New Jersey. His first post in a church came in 1766, when he was called to Windham, where he became a pastor, spending the rest of his life in town.

While in Windham, the couple had seven more children, including their seventh child, Simon-Finley. Simon Williams passed away on November 10, 1793; his wife survived him by almost twelve years, dying on July 28, 1805.

Simon-Finley grew up in Windham and eventually married Mary Gregg, who also resided in town. Like his father, Simon-Finley became a very educated man, graduating from Dartmouth College at the age of twenty-one in 1785. Following in the footsteps of his father, he took up the clerical profession, being ordained in Methuen, Massachusetts, on December 13, 1786. However, he left the church in Methuen soon after because, according to Leonard Morrison, "his mind became unsettled; he had trouble with his church." The exact nature of this trouble is unknown to this day, but one particularly interesting stanza of his final sermon there has been recorded for posterity:

Oh, might I fly to change my place,
How would I choose to dwell
In some wide, lonesome wilderness,
And leave these gates of hell.

The cause of his departure from Methuen was certainly not a distaste for a clerical occupation because Williams found himself a job at a church in Meredith, New Hampshire, shortly after. Although it is unknown what his salary was in Methuen, the people of Meredith surely felt his services were of value. They offered him a generous salary of sixty pounds, only twenty of which was to be paid in cash. Another third of the salary was to be paid in corn and other grains, and the rest was to be paid in beef and pork. His post did not last more than five years before there was turmoil between Williams and the church.

In 1797, Williams was dismissed from his position and excommunicated. This time a record was made regarding the nature of his dismissal; there were charges made against him concerning his moral character. However, there are no available records about the exact nature of the charges, so it is up to the reader to imagine what Reverend Williams might have been guilty of. Shortly after being excommunicated, Williams abandoned his family and joined the U.S. Navy, serving aboard the USS *Essex* as either a ship's steward or chaplain, depending on which records one consults.

In the summer of 1800, the ship reached Batavia, the modern-day capital of Indonesia, Jakarta. His superiors on the frigate knew of his clerical background and arranged for Williams to give an oration aboard the ship on the occasion of the Fourth of July. However, Williams was suddenly stricken with fever and died the day before he had planned to give his speech. He was given a proper burial at sea, and his family was notified of his untimely passing.

The widowed Mary Gregg did not wait long before marrying again, this time to John Anderson of Windham. A long time passed, and the couple grew old together, enjoying a relatively uneventful life. However, this was soon changed with the arrival of a man who would become the center of one of the greatest mysteries of Windham's history. Although no one knew where he came from or why he came to Windham, these were not the deepest of the mysteries surrounding him.

While he was reluctant to reveal the details of his past or anything personal in nature, he was much more willing to give detailed accounts of Windham's history to anyone who inquired. How could a stranger have been so acquainted with the history of a town he had seemingly never visited before? This was not the only thing the people he interacted with, and people to this day, find surprising. The stranger was well versed with the history and intimate details of the Williams family, the family of the late Reverend Simon-Finley Williams.

While in town, the stranger moved about in what Morrison described as "a mysterious manner," yet he did not wish to avoid detection, as he visited many people. One of those the man was interested in paying a visit to was the elderly Mary Anderson, the widow of Reverend Simon-Finley Williams. Whatever was discussed between them is lost to history, as Anderson steadfastly refused to disclose any information about her conversation with the stranger, nor any details he may have revealed to her about his own identity.

The stranger left town soon after speaking with Mrs. Anderson, leaving Windham as mysteriously and as suddenly as he entered. No one in town ever saw the man again, but those who were familiar with Reverend Simon-Finley Williams were adamant the stranger who came to town was the late reverend, a man who had been dead—his body supposedly deep below the ocean—for decades.

7

BUILDING NORTH LOWELL ROAD

The first roads in Windham, as well as those in colonial New England in general, were nothing more than mere dirt paths worn by the passing of early settlers. Trees along a path were often marked so that those unfamiliar with the territory would be able to find their way. However, it was not long before the first official roads were laid out in the area of Londonderry that became Windham. Many times, the roads were built along the old paths, as these paths would have likely been clear of most major obstacles, such as large rocks and trees. However, when debris was present, clearing the road proved to be a very difficult task. The clearing of brush, trees and boulders was often done by hand or with horses in the case of particularly large, heavy obstacles. Although the well-built roads of larger towns were often leveled for the convenience of those traveling on them, the early roads of Windham were rather crude.

In fact, many of the roads in colonial Windham were barely passable for horses. As carriages and horse-drawn carts did not exist in Windham at the time, it was unnecessary to improve the roads sufficiently for such vehicles. There is an interesting story about one of the first animal-drawn vehicles to ride along the roads of Windham. The local deacon decided it would be to his advantage if he constructed an ox-drawn cart for himself. He started by cutting down a large maple tree, which was then sawed into pieces in order to serve as wheels. Holes were bored through the center of each wheel for an axle. The rather crude vehicle had one unfortunate drawback. Every time the wheels made a single revolution, they would emit a horrible screeching sound that could be heard for some distance.

Although the deacon seemed not to mind the noise—at least, not enough to cease using the cart—one of his neighbors certainly did. On one morning in particular, the neighbor was greeted with the horrendous sound of the wheels of the oxcart. There was no apparent explanation for the bizarre noise, and he was quick to attribute them to something of the supernatural realm. He thought Judgment Day was approaching, and even though he was not a particularly pious man, he ran into his house and began to read his Bible. He spent the entire day reading from the scriptures and praying. However, toward the evening, a friend who lived nearby arrived at his home, and their conversation began with the deacon's neighbor asking his acquaintance if he had heard any noise out of the ordinary. In reply, the friend said that the only noise he had heard that day was the deacon's new oxcart.

The first official road laid out in Windham was approved by the town on November 6, 1742. The new highway began near Golden Brook and went on to follow the route of an older path. Several other major roads were also constructed in town between the 1740s and the first quarter of the nineteenth century. One such road was the one leading from the northeastern section of Windham to the town center. However, there was not one single extensive road that would be akin to the modern North Lowell Road. Rather, the road was a network of several roads, which meandered their way to the town center. One such subset of the road was built between the properties of John Hemphill and Agnes Hemphill. When the time came to construct such a road in the 1820s, the builders were met with a dilemma.

Although hard labor and horse-drawn implements often proved sufficient to remove many of the obstacles in the paths of new roads, the path between the Hemphill homes was interrupted by a hill. The hill being too large to cut through or remove completely, the town was left having to decide whether or not the road should be constructed around the hill or over the hill. Eventually, it was decided the short stretch of road should be built around the hill, making it easier for the horses and pedestrians who would be using the road.

For the next several years, the town received numerous petitions asking for the antecedent of North Lowell Road to be straightened and widened. However, the town declined to do so on each occasion. Eventually, the road commissioners were notified, and the older part of the road was widened and a new stretch of road added. To widen the road would have required

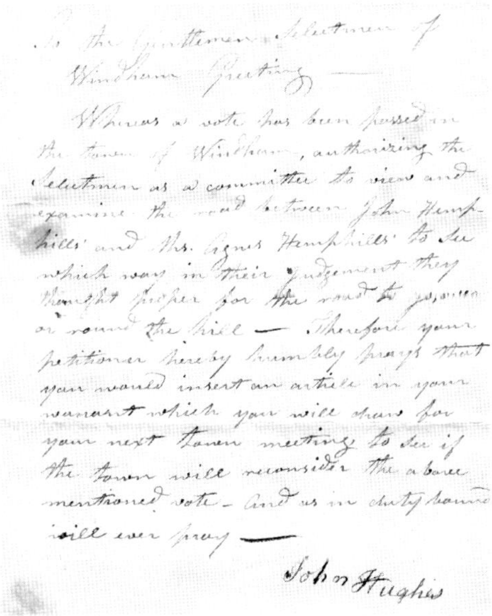

To the Gentlemen Selectmen of
Windham Greeting —
Whereas a vote has been passed in
the town of Windham, authorizing the
Selectmen as a committee to view and
examine the road between John Hemp-
hill and Mrs. Agnes Hemphills to see
which way in their judgement they
thought proper for the road to go, over
or round the hill — Therefore your
petitioner hereby humbly prays that
you would insert an article in your
warrant which you will draw for
your next town meeting to see if
the town will reconsider the above
mentioned vote — And as in duty bound
will ever pray —
John Hughes

An 1820s petition to build a road "over or round the hill" to connect two nearby Hemphill properties. *Author's collection.*

the clearing of much of the natural obstacles that may have been off to the side of the old road. Also, straightening the road was surely a monumental feat for the day. Without modern surveying instruments, laborers would have had to straighten the entire length of the road based on rough estimates.

The completed highway began at the property of John Hemphill and continued south for about 1,500 feet. Although there were certainly residents living north of the Hemphill property, no improvements were made to connect their roads with the new road. However, they would have certainly had to make use of the new road to reach the town center. The stretch of the road that began at the home of John Hemphill eventually met a preexisting road that continued on to the town's meetinghouse. When the highway was completed, the road was about 50 feet wide, allowing for horse-drawn vehicles to safely share the road with pedestrians.

As with many modern-day roads and infrastructure projects, it was necessary to cut through the private land of several property owners along the route. John Cochran received the lion's share of damages from the town, which amounted to $266.00. Another property owner received just $12.00. Windham spent an additional $39.69 on building the road itself; the entire project cost only $317.69. With the costs of many modern roads exceeding many millions, it is hard to imagine that, at one time, a road could be built for such a nominal sum. Also, the costs were certainly reduced by not cutting through the hill, a decision that might have been very different in the current century.

8

BUTTERFIELD'S BOULDER

No one is completely sure of the origin of the moniker that was given to the large glacial erratic more than a century ago, although it was certainly named for a man by the name of Butterfield. The nearly twenty-foot-high granite boulder is far different from any of the rocks in its vicinity. The rock is one of the largest freestanding boulders in New Hampshire and has rested in its current position for thousands upon thousands of years. Much can be learned about the boulder's prehistoric history by observation. As interest in the boulder increased in the nineteenth century, townspeople began to become interested in how the unusual landmark came to be. One period observation suggested that the smoothness of the exposed cavity was likely the result of pebbles being forced against the stone by a strong current. More evidence of its ancient origins can be found in several fracture marks along the upper ledge of the boulder. These marks were made from the vast sheets of ice that spanned the entirety of the country and beyond during the glacial age. It is the glacial ice that was the driving force behind depositing the boulder where it now stands on one of Windham's highest hills.

As for its unique shape, the *Portsmouth Herald* once referred to the boulder as "resembling the gigantic skull of some prehistoric monster." Geologists who have studied the rock over the past century have arrived at the conclusion that it did not originally form near Windham and was likely originally located a significant distance away. It has also been established that the boulder has likely rested upside down for the thousands of years it has been in Windham. The evidence for this is a small "basin" on what is now the underside of the

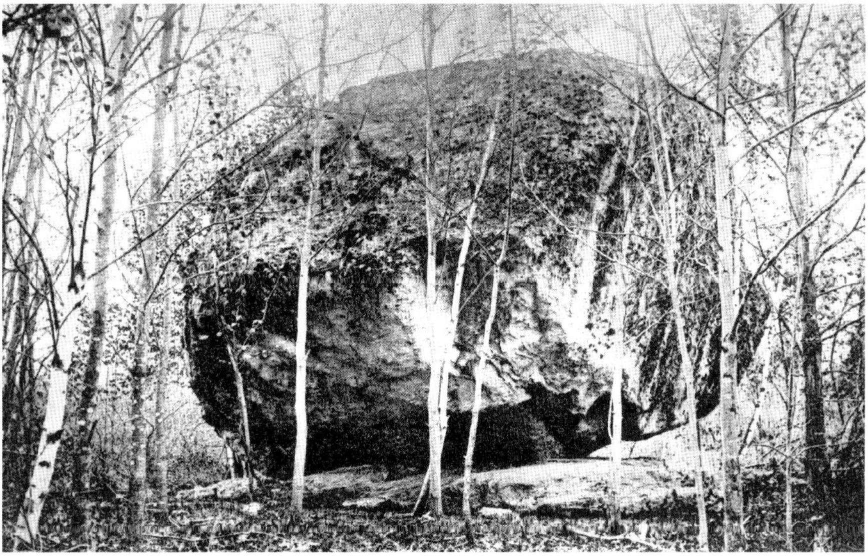

Butterfield's Boulder as it appeared in 1883, around the time townspeople began to become interested in the massive boulder. *From* History of Windham in New Hampshire (Rockingham County), 1719–1883.

boulder. This provides ample room for curious visitors to stick their heads in and say a few words; the natural acoustic qualities provide a similar effect to speaking into "a brass kettle."

Many have speculated since the nineteenth century that the rock took its name from a man from Chelmsford, Massachusetts, with the surname Butterfield. While he did not reside or own land in Windham, he did have land near the original Nutfield settlement, and there is no one else by that name in the area at the time the rock was first known by its current moniker. However, the legend of the rock does not end with the debate over the origin of the name. Rather, the boulder gained notoriety in town due to the legend of a hunter by the name of Butterfield who used the rock as shelter on his many hunting trips in Windham.

Like much of the history of Butterfield's Boulder, there is almost nothing known about the hunter who traversed the woods of Windham and stopped at the boulder to make his camp. The cavity under the boulder would have provided the perfect opening for the hunter to use as a shelter when night approached. Butterfield would have hunted in the early days of Windham's settlement. This was a time when bears were common, and even if Butterfield did not intentionally seek to hunt the animal, he would

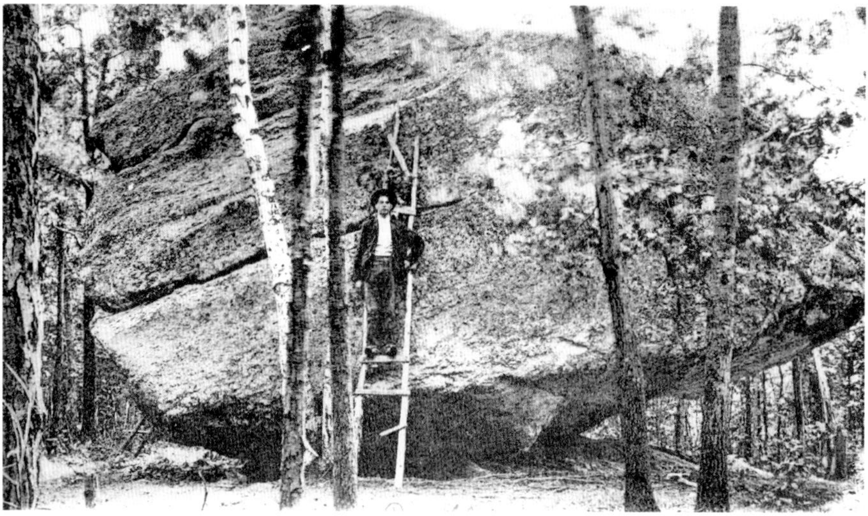

A souvenir postcard showing a man on a ladder against Butterfield's Boulder. *Author's collection.*

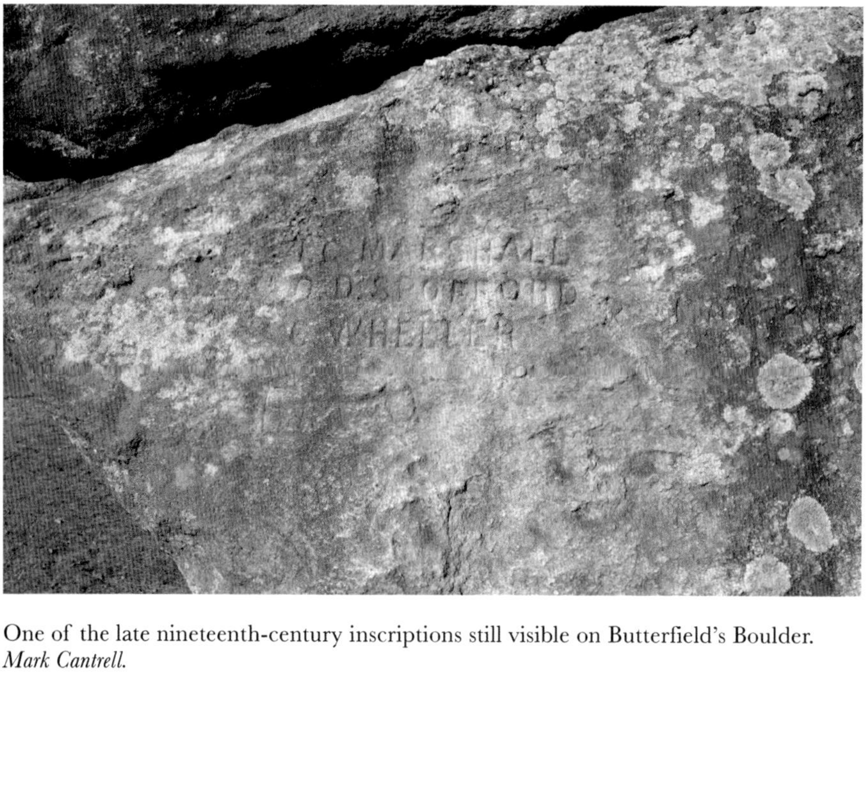

One of the late nineteenth-century inscriptions still visible on Butterfield's Boulder. *Mark Cantrell.*

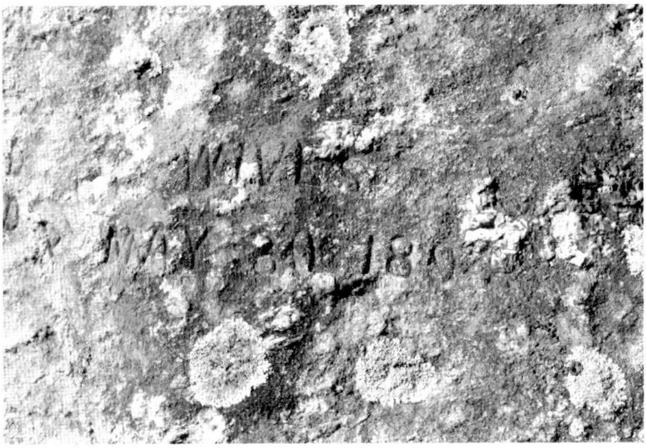

Inscription on Butterfield's Boulder dated May 30, 1894. *Mark Cantrell.*

have likely taken the proper precautions to ensure his night's slumber was not interrupted by a curious bear. Another wild animal Butterfield likely would have encountered but that is no longer common is the wolf. Several of the eighteenth-century settlers noted how bothersome the wolves were, and the community would likely have been better off if Butterfield had slain one of the animals on occasion.

However, it is not the story of the hunter alone that resulted in Butterfield's Boulder gaining in popularity. At the turn of the twentieth century, it was discovered that the top of the boulder made for a great viewing platform of the scenery around it. The top of the rock was level enough that maneuvering there would not be a precarious feat. As the boulder is about forty feet in length, it would have provided room for several people to enjoy the view from the top at the same time. In order to reach the top, a makeshift wooden ladder was often available, but this ascent was likely quite intimidating to those worried about the stability of the ladder or climbing to such a height. Those who did reach the top were rewarded with a view of Windham unlike any other.

Rather than carve one's initials into a tree, where they would likely eventually disappear with time, several young teenagers from a century ago took the time to carve an inscription into Butterfield's Boulder. Several young boys made the effort to carve their first initials and entire last names into the rock. As the inscriptions are still visible to this day, the boys would certainly be proud to know they left a lasting mark on Windham. There is also another easily readable inscription that is dated from May 1894. Eventually, the popularity of Butterfield's Boulder declined, along with the popularity of other natural tourist attractions.

9

THE RAILROAD COMES TO WINDHAM

Although extensive railway systems began to appear in the United States as early as the first decades of the nineteenth century, it would be years before this revolutionary technology connected the nation's rural towns to larger cities. Railroads came through small, isolated towns with promises of a more efficient method for farmers and local craftsman to bring their products to market. Once travel by railroad became commonplace decades later, the railway systems that were already in place allowed for a convenient way for those living in rural towns, such as Windham, to go to the city for the day or just visit friends a couple towns over.

The first railroad to lay its tracks in Windham was the Manchester & Lawrence Railroad, which first came to town in 1848. After a year of construction, the railroad was open for business in 1849; the first train to ride along the newly laid tracks did so on November 11 of that year. As the train was to stop in Windham, a station was erected on the west side of the tracks where two existing roads crossed. A cattle pass had to be built under the tracks so the cattle of a nearby farmer could safely cross the road. From this station, the train would have continued on toward the town line between Windham and Salem near Canobie Lake. When the track was laid at this section of town, the crew ran into difficulty as they were forced to cut through rock. To do so required many hours of hard labor with hand tools, as well as primitive blasting technology using nothing but black powder.

A much different problem occurred when workmen began laying track near Mitchell's Pond. The roadbed happened to be over an old meadow, and as such, the ground was not very firm. The road would continually sink, requiring a persistent effort on the part of the workmen to continually fill in the area beneath the bed until at last the ground was solid enough to support the weight of a train.

The Manchester & Lawrence operated independently for just under one year before it was leased to the Concord Railway, but it reverted back to independent ownership after a few years. However, it was not long before the railway was again leased by several other railways, and it was ultimately leased by the Boston & Maine Railroad for fifty years; the Boston & Maine purchased the Manchester & Lawrence outright in 1919 through a stock exchange.

However, the Manchester & Lawrence was not the only line to come through Windham. Through a series of consolidations and leases beginning in 1848, the Nashua & Epping Railroad eventually made its way through Windham in 1874 after being leased by the Worcester & Nashua Railroad. Before the construction was even started on the Worcester & Nashua Railroad, the company had leased the Nashua & Rochester Railroad for a term of fifty years. In 1883, the two railroads merged to become the Worcester, Nashua & Rochester Railroad. As the Boston & Maine began to dominate the region, as well as much of the Northeast, the railroad conglomerate leased the Worcester, Nashua & Rochester and later purchased it in 1911. Although the Boston & Maine eventually dominated the railroads of Windham, one cannot overlook the history of the railways in Windham prior to the Boston & Maine.

When the Nashua & Rochester Railroad laid its track through Windham, the route crossed over the already existing route of the Manchester & Lawrence. Although this occurred just under four hundred feet from the preexisting Windham station, a new station was built by the Nashua & Rochester to accommodate a greater amount of passengers. The new $2,200 station was composed of two equal-sized wings, each of which had a waiting room for the passengers. The old station was later moved about two hundred feet and was no longer used by passengers. Instead, it became a general purpose building, at times serving as a home for the gate crossing attendant and his family. On the occasion of a layover where railway workers or others were stuck in Windham for a night, they would be offered the opportunity to board at the former train station.

As trains were routinely passing through Windham to deliver and pick up freight, it was necessary for Windham Junction to have a freight house. It is recorded that in 1869, an old passenger station from Salem was brought to

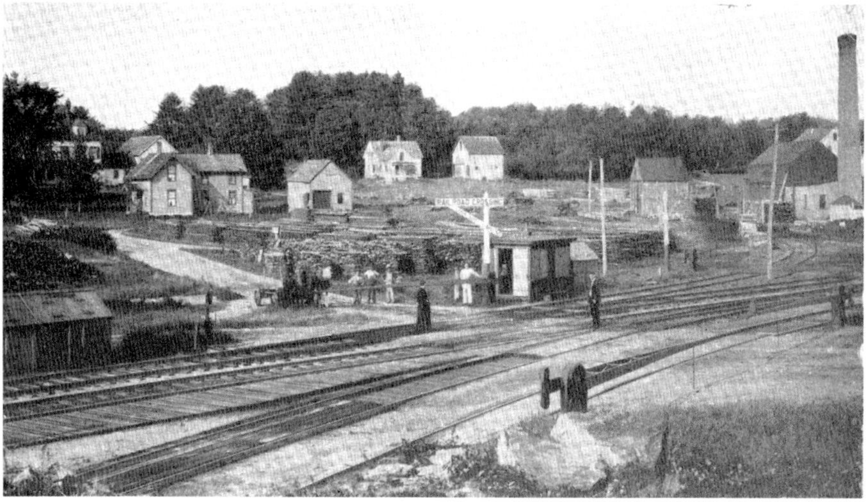

A postcard view of Windham Junction as it appeared circa 1910. *Author's collection.*

Windham Junction and refurbished to store freight, as well as the handcars. It is believed that this building was later used as a grain store when more modern buildings were constructed near the site. The growth of the railroad also required the construction of other structures, including a water tank. When the first water tank in Windham was constructed in the latter part of the nineteenth century, it was relatively short, with legs that were only ten feet high. Sometime around the turn of the twentieth century, it was raised in order to meet railroad standards.

Businesses, as well as a post office, were built so that they were in proximity of the town's railroad stations. When Edwin Stickney built his store in 1861, his property became one of the most extensive structures along the railway; it included the general store, a barn and several attached horse sheds. Stickney not only ran a rather successful business but also left his mark on the railroad industry. He was responsible for the construction of two crossings designed for where the railroad crosses another road; the roads being Frost and Depot Road. Eventually such crossings were designated as "Stickney's" in the timetables issued to the employees of the Boston & Maine.

George Seavey also took advantage of the railroad and built his sawmill near the tracks of the Manchester & Lawrence in 1868. However, the building burned several years later; it was rebuilt in 1877, and the new mill was larger than its predecessor. Its sixty-five-foot-tall square brick chimney rose high above anything that had been constructed in Windham at the

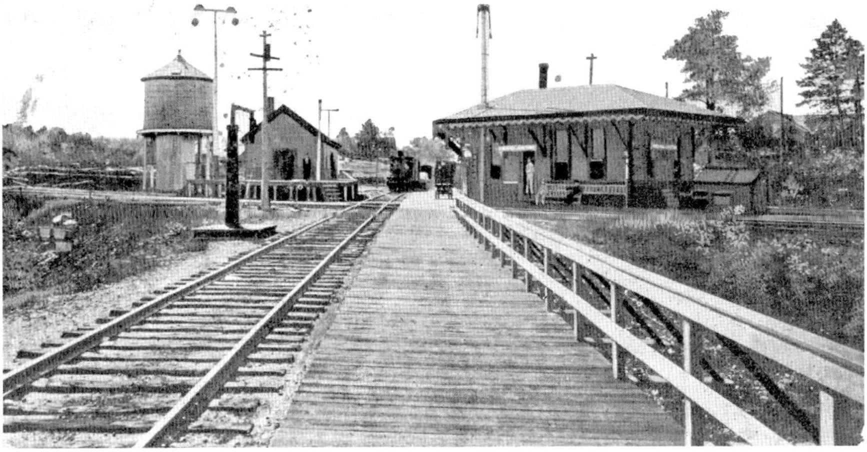

An early postcard view of the depot at Windham Junction. Notice the train approaching the station. *Author's collection.*

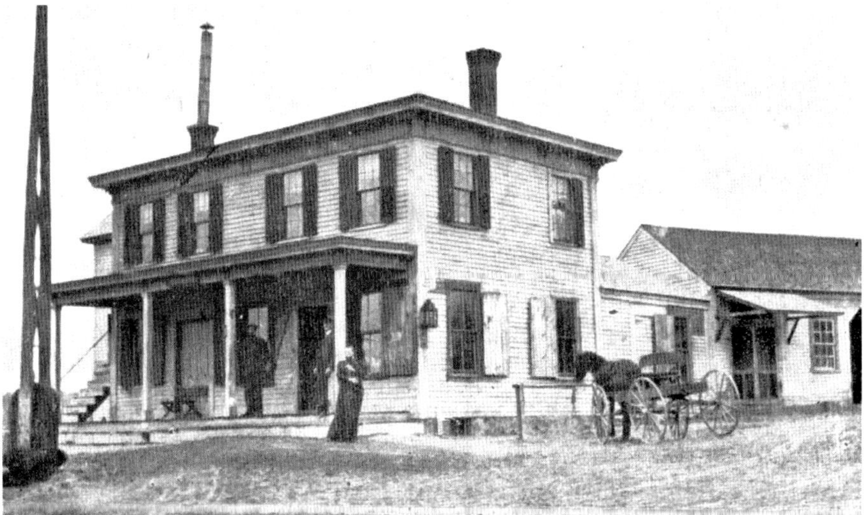

Circa 1910 view of Stickney's general store at Windham Junction. *Author's collection.*

time, making it a striking symbol of Seavey's business. The nearby railroad would have allowed Seavey to easily ship his lumber to interested buyers. Seavey later opened a cider mill on the site, a business that thrived with easy access to railways that could ship the cider to larger cities and towns.

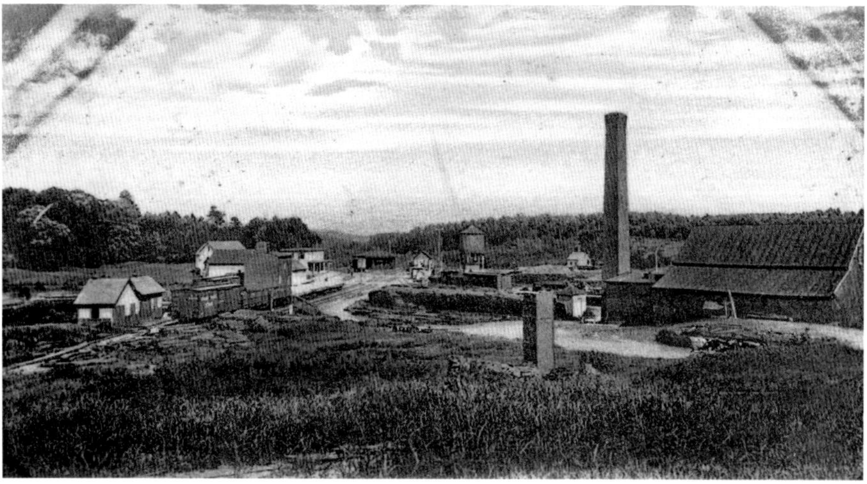

Early postcard of George Seavey's mill complex at Windham Junction showing the six-story brick chimney. *Author's collection.*

His prominence in town helped him to draw support when he worked with other people of influence in order to prevent shoe factories from being built near Windham Junction. Seavey, along with others, was able to convince the local landowners to not sell their land, and the shoe companies were forced to build their factories farther north in Derry. The shoe industry was responsible for much of the industrial development in that town.

When the dairy industry in town began to become sizeable in the last quarter of the nineteenth century, a milk car was added to the railway in order to transport much of the milk produced in Windham. Local farmers were able to bring their milk to the nearest train station, where it would eventually be delivered to the H.P. Hood facility in South Lawrence. One local dairy farm, the Lamson farm, utilized the railway to transport the milk and other products produced at the farm to the Lamson store in Boston. Not only was the refrigerated car far superior to early deliveries made by horse-drawn carriages, but the train car was also able to transport more in much less time.

In 1910, the "Junction" in Windham Junction was officially removed from the name, and the station became known simply by the name of the town in which it stood. The station agent there usually had two operators who worked with him in order to perform the necessary duties of running a train station. At one point, both of the operators were women, an occurrence that is not recorded as happening anywhere else along the Boston & Maine line prior to that time. A train collision near West Windham Station in 1907 resulted in the name of that station being changed to Anderson Station in order to avoid confusion with the other Windham station. This was likely helpful in preventing another accident.

When the Bar Harbor Express opened in 1902 as a joint venture between the Boston & Maine and other railroads, the line passed through Windham for a decade of consecutive summers. When the train would pass by the Windham station, many nearby families would wake up their children early in the morning and bring them down to see the train that carried the millionaires. As Bar Harbor was a popular summer retreat for the wealthy in the Northeast, it would not be uncommon for well-known millionaires from New York or Massachusetts to ride as passengers on the train. However, this tradition did not last long, as the Bar Harbor Express was rerouted around Windham in 1912.

In 1927, a fire broke out at the general store at the Junction that destroyed the store and all of the attached buildings. The store's proprietor and postmaster, Otis Clyde, rebuilt the store to sell groceries, as well as a small stock of other essential items. When cars became more commonplace in Windham, gasoline pumps were installed, and this was a rather successful

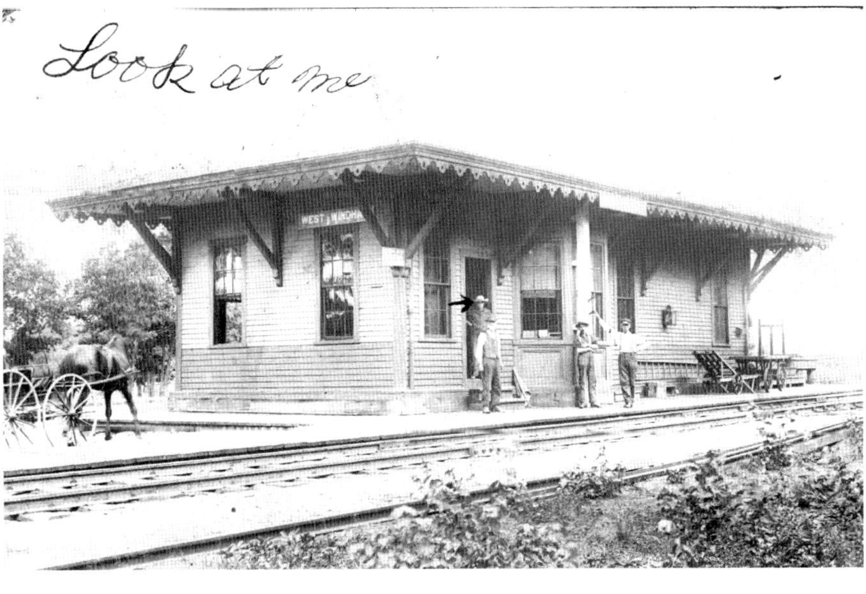

The station at West Windham, later known as Anderson Station. The station agent and railway workers can be seen in front of the station. *Author's collection.*

business for Clyde. However, the store was short-lived and was closed in 1945; the structure was torn down two decades later.

At the same time, the railroad service through Windham was also beginning to fade out. By the 1930s, freight service had been discontinued, and passenger service was even reduced to just a single round trip once a day, save for Sunday. A passenger train stopped in Windham for the last time on July 10, 1953. By this time, most residents had access to a car, and the town and state roads were adequate enough for fairly efficient, easy travel by automobile.

10

THE MAN WHO SAVED WINDHAM'S HISTORY

Writing local histories was not a common practice in antebellum America. Undoubtedly, many of the unique stories and persons of small, rural towns have been lost to the ages simply because they were never written down; oral tradition alone was not enough to carry them through the passage of centuries. Fortunately, by the last quarter of the nineteenth century, small-town authors began to publish histories of their hometowns. Not focusing on any one aspect of history in particular, an author would seek to write about everything in town, preserving otherwise ephemeral anecdotes and important pieces of local history for the generations to come. Those researching Windham's history in modern times have greatly benefitted from the "bible" of Windham history, Leonard A. Morrison's *History of Windham in New Hampshire (Rockingham County), 1719–1883*. Morrison's book provided an account of the town's history from its settlement in 1719 until the time it was published in 1883.

The Morrison family's pedigree can be traced back to the early sixth century when three Morrison brothers, Fergus, Lorn and Angus, left Ireland for the western coast of Scotland. Leonard Morrison gives a short, yet interesting, account of how his surname originated:

> *In 787, these* [the western coast and nearby islands] *were attacked by the sons of Morgue, which means "a man from the sea." They were of Norse-viking race. One of the daughters of Morgue married Kenneth Mhor, or More, who lived in Lewis, and came from Glen Moreson in West*

> *Lothian, Scotland, where a battle was fought in the year 640,—Mhor, Mhoir, or More, Meaning "big or large man." This battle was called "the battle of Big sons of big men in the Glen," hence the name of "Glen Mhoireson," or Glen Morrison."*

When the charter for Nutfield was issued in 1719, five of the Morrison men of Scotland found themselves belonging to the group of 119 persons who became the founders of modern Derry, Londonderry and Windham, the five men being Robert, David, Samuel, James and John. John Morrison, the father of the John on the town charter, is the patriarch ancestor of the Nutfield branch of the Morrison family. Believed to have been born around 1628 in Aberdeen, Scotland, Morrison removed to Londonderry, Ireland, sometime before the siege of the city took place in 1688. He and his family survived the siege, and his sons made their way to the Nutfield region of New Hampshire in 1719. John followed his sons, immigrating to Londonderry sometime shortly after 1720. It is reported that he died at the age of 108 in 1736, though there is insufficient information to prove he lived to such an advanced age.

Although John is the patriarchal ancestor of the Morrison family in Nutfield, Lieutenant Samuel Morrison was the progenitor of the family in Windham. He came to town sometime around 1730, shortly after it was laid out, and quickly became involved in local politics. Samuel held a range of positions, including moderator at the first town meeting, town clerk and selectman. There are, of course, countless more ancestors of Leonard A. Morrison who can be found in the annals of town history, many of whom were prominent in the local community. From a Revolutionary War soldier with a remarkable battle story to one of the earliest supporters of the antislavery cause, the Morrison who came to the rescue of Windham's history certainly had an impressive pedigree to live up to.

Leonard Allison Morrison was born in Windham on February 21, 1843. As a child, Morrison experienced the untimely death of his brothers and was also left with many of the tasks essential to the running of the household due to the poor health of his parents. Despite the time spent taking care of family matters, he was able to obtain education at the schoolhouses of Windham and go on to become a learned man. After completing rudimentary schooling in Windham, Morrison left for Gowanda, New York, to study at the Union School. After returning from New York, he attended the New Hampshire Conference Seminary, which is located in what is now the town of Tilton, New Hampshire. However, Morrison was not satisfied with the traditional education he had received through his years spent in the classroom. Thus, he decided he would supplement the education he had received with self-education obtained by "intercourse with the world" and through private studies. Looking back on his studies, Morrison recollected that he "was always fond of reading… and in [books] found companionship, solace, and delight."

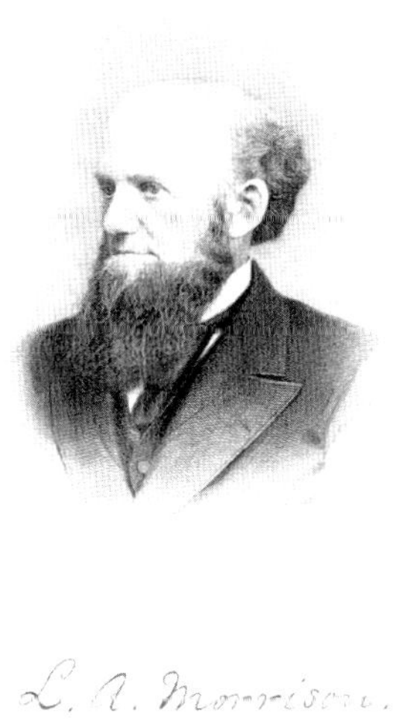

An 1883 engraving of Leonard A. Morrison with a facsimile signature. *From* History of Windham in New Hampshire (Rockingham County), 1719–1883.

His love for the written word was not limited to reading. Morrison began contributing to several newspapers at the age of eighteen. Morrison's thirst for writing was not quenched through his occasional newspaper editorials, though. In 1878, he began work on a book on a subject close to his heart: the history of his own family. First published in 1880, period reviews note that the book was well received, and copies had even made their way to the family's homeland, Scotland. It was after he finished *History of the Morison, or Morrison, Family* that he began one of his life's most important undertakings—preserving the history of Windham, the town his family had called home for over a century.

There had been no extensive work on the history of Windham published before *History of Windham in New Hampshire* in 1883. In fact, Morrison lamented that by the time he began writing about the town's history, it was "too late." He knew that "a history should have been written fifty years ago." Even in 1880, many pieces of the town's early history had certainly been lost with the passing of generations. The older members of the community held with them recollections of interactions with early settlers and the important events of the founding of the town. However, without a strong oral tradition, those memories faded away and can never be replaced. For this reason, Morrison dedicated more than three years of his life compiling every birth record in town, spending countless hours at the local cemeteries and visiting many of the old cellar holes in town.

When Morrison's monumental undertaking was completed, the result was more than just a book. The tome of over eight hundred pages was set in a simple Victorian cloth binding. As the market was relatively limited, only 725 copies of the book were printed. The only mention of the sale price of the book is that when it was discovered only $300 of the $400 allotted by the town to "aid in the publication" of the book was needed, the price was adjusted accordingly in a ratio to the $300. The town also provided $200 for views of landscapes in town to be added to the book. As the book also provided extensive genealogical records, including those of almost every person to have ever resided in Windham up to the date of publication, the many portraits of various local persons were placed in the book at the expense of the person themselves or their family. In total, it is noted that over $2,400 was spent illustrating the work; in 2016 dollars, this would be approximately $58,000. In his introduction, Morrison wrote that "every copy of the *History of Windham, N.H.*, contains more than it was advertised to contain."

Leonard Allison Morrison's legacy to his hometown is of immeasurable proportions; no one has ever contributed so much in the interest of the history of Windham. Almost everything known beyond the unadorned facts of Windham prior to 1883 would have been lost to history were it not for Morrison. The story of how Windham's early history was preserved is not just of local relevance. It speaks volumes about the importance of recording history and ensuring local and regional history is kept alive for generations and centuries to come.

11

WALLACE FESSENDEN

Eight hundred spectators filled Pittsburgh's Recreation Park even though the threat of rain loomed on the horizon. On that day in June 1889, two of the National League's finest teams, the Pittsburgh Alleghenys and the Washington Senators, met each other on the field. By the third inning, the Alleghenys had done a remarkable job of giving themselves an advantage, almost assuring the home team of a win in the eyes of the fans. However, with rain drizzling on the field, the Senators were able to tie up the score in the fourth inning. As the Senators' sudden success was seemingly timed with the rain, the Pittsburgh fans saw the rain as a "curse" on their team.

However, as the rain fell even harder, the home team was able to garner two more runs in the first half of the fifth inning. The crowd no longer saw the rain as a curse. Instead, "everybody was delighted that the rain was so prolific and threatening," according to the *Pittsburg Dispatch*. Despite no sign of the rain letting up, the umpire yelled, "Play ball!" steadfastly refusing to end the game. A reporter for the newspaper also noted that as the rain continued to pour down, "up went groans from the bleaching board crowds that were concealed under umbrellas." The umpire who was met with groans of disapproval from the crowd was none other than Windham's own Wallace Fessenden.

Stephen Fessenden was the first of his family to reside in Windham, moving to town from Boston in about 1830. Fessenden had been a hardware merchant in Boston for several years before his father purchased Isaac Senter's mill in Windham. The saw- and gristmill was purchased as a gift for

Stephen. When he arrived with his family, he wasted no time in erecting a new shingle and clapboard mill, as well as a building for carding rolls, which would have been necessary for wool production. However, Fessenden soon branched out into new business pursuits, expanding his mill operation to include the manufacture of flannels. His business acumen, or lack thereof, is recorded in the *History of Windham in New Hampshire (Rockingham County), 1719–1883*:

> *He was not a successful manufacturer nor a good financier. He seemed to have but little idea of the value of money,—when he had it, it was used freely; and When he was short of it, he was too free in contracting debts, and making Promises of payment which it was impossible for him to fulfil* [sic].

Fortunately, Fessenden mended his ways later in life and became much more prosperous and happy. His business was responsible for the employment of about thirty individuals in the community, many of whom were forced to find work elsewhere after his death. Stephen and his wife, Caroline, had twelve children between 1820 and 1836. Interestingly, Caroline gave birth to two sets of twins on two separate occasions. On May 10, 1831, she gave birth to Joshua Allan and Caroline Elizabeth; Joshua died just over a year later, while Caroline Elizabeth lived an average, healthy life. Exactly two years after the date of the birth of her first set of twins, Caroline gave birth to her second set of twins, Benjamin and Nancy. Benjamin died the day after his birth and Nancy died a day later.

Stephen's and Caroline's eldest son, David, enlisted in Company C of the Thirteenth New Hampshire Volunteer Regiment during the Civil War. Although he had a mostly unremarkable career in fighting for the Union, David did see action at the Battle of Fredericksburg. David did not have any children with his first wife, Susan Smith, and it is unknown how that marriage ended. Alice Sellars of Castine, Maine, was David's second wife, with whom he raised a family in Windham.

Wallace Clifton Fessenden was born on October 5, 1860, to parents David and Alice Fessenden. Although relatively little is known about Wallace's childhood, it is likely he relocated to Lynn, Massachusetts, with his family sometime as a young child. Whether or not he was first exposed to the game of baseball in Windham or Lynn is unknown, but his earliest recorded involvement with baseball was as a player and manager for the Lynn team of the Massachusetts State Association in 1884. Fessenden was also the manager of the Salem, Massachusetts team of the New England League. The New England League was an association of minor-league baseball teams throughout the New England region. Originally the Salem Fairies, the team changed its name to the Salem Witches in 1888, the new name being more reflective of Salem's past.

In 1889, Fessenden became an umpire for the National League, umpiring a total of fifty-three games over the span of two seasons. One of the games was the Pittsburgh versus Washington matchup that took place on June 25, 1889, despite the rain. Moving into the first half of the sixth inning, no additional runs were scored by the home team. As the home team's last batter struck out, there were demands from the team that the game be called due to the downpour. Despite their pleas to end the game, Arthur Irwin went up to bat for the Senators in the second half of the sixth inning.

Following the rules of nineteenth-century American baseball, two strikes had been called against the Senators before Fessenden decided to call the game. The *Pittsburg Dispatch* reported that the umpire's decision was the "wisest [ruling] he has made during his visit here." In the certainly biased opinion of Pittsburgh fans, Fessenden had routinely made close calls in favor of the Senators, appearing as though he favored the visiting team. Despite what was thought of Fessenden's apparent impartiality, the Alleghenys ended the game with a seven-to-five win over the Senators.

This was not the first game in which Fessenden's calls were questioned. In the summer of 1888, the *Saint Paul Daily Globe* took a jab at Fessenden's umpiring with the headline "Even Umpire Fessenden Couldn't Prevent Apostles from Winning." Clearly the Saint Paul sportswriter took issue with Fessenden despite his team's win over the Kansas City Blues. Even with home field advantage, the Blues were consistently outplayed, and the Apostles remained in the lead for the entirety of the game. However, a simple victory was seemingly not satisfactory for the fans of the Apostles, as the *Saint Paul Daily Globe* reported that "had it not been for some costly errors and miserable decisions by the umpire, Fessenden, the Blues would have been treated with a coat of whitewash." The newspaper reporter accused Fessenden of letting four runs by the Apostles go unrecorded. Not that those four runs truly mattered, as the Apostles won the game with a six-run lead, the final score being ten to four.

On another occasion, Fessenden was accused of aiding the visiting team by not being fully familiarized with the rules of the Northwestern League. However, Fessenden's contribution to the world of baseball is not limited to his career as an umpire. He is credited with discovering one of baseball's all-time greats, Hall of Famer Hugh Duffy. In fact, it is recorded that Fessenden took pride in his self-proclaimed talent for discovering unrecognized talent. Unfortunately for Fessenden, one of the backers of the team he managed did not have much money to invest in the club, and when money was spent, it was wasted foolishly. Instead of investing money in hiring better players and signing them to lucrative but fair contracts, the money was spent in attempts to make the existing players better. Such expenditures were relatively unsuccessful, and Fessenden was left begging for more money to hire better players.

When Duffy was chosen by Fessenden to play for the Salem Fairies in 1886, he was provided with twenty-five dollars upfront as well as five dollars a week plus boarding, terms the team's backer had to be persuaded to agree to. If Duffy's rookie game was an indication of his talent, the investment would prove to be a poor one. As an outfielder, Duffy missed several balls and fumbled around the field making other mistakes. After that game, both Duffy and Fessenden were fired, but in a stroke of luck, the team was sold that night. The new owner welcomed the two back for a second chance.

The new owner could not have regretted his decision. Duffy went on to hit a home run and played exceptionally well as an outfielder in that second game. Although Duffy played professionally until 1906, he was in the prime of his career in 1894, when he played for the Boston Beaneaters. During that season he set the record, which still stands, for the highest single season batting average; Duffy ended the season with just under a .440. His involvement in baseball continued until the last years of his life, and in 1945, he was inducted into the Hall of Fame.

Wallace Fessenden's baseball career was not nearly as long. After retiring from umpiring in the early 1890s, he became involved in horse racing. By the early 1900s, Fessenden was making a fortune with his race horses. Most notably, in 1903, a Thoroughbred horse he owned, Pass Book, won him $50,000 at the Jamaica track; the sum would be equivalent to over $1.3 million in 2016. At a race at the Aqueduct track in 1904, Pass Book won another $30,000. However, Fessenden might have been so successful with Pass Book only due to a well-planned lie. It was reported that Fessenden had been responsible for spreading a report about Pass Book being in poor health due to suffering through a bad winter. While this report was making its way around bet-making circles, Fessenden worked to convince a few of his Wall Street broker friends to bet on Pass Book at odds of one hundred to one.

Shortly before the race, Pass Book received special training to ensure he would be able to compensate for the possibility of an unskilled jockey. Any such worries were certainly abated when one of the best riders in the country was hired for the race. On the day of the race, the Wall Street men went around placing small bets of just ten or twenty dollars at odds of between fifty to one and thirty to one. However, so many bets were placed that the odds eventually dropped to about ten to one. When the race was over and Pass Book was victorious, it is reported that the trainers of the other horses grew tired of watching Fessenden counting his many thousands of dollars.

Fessenden's winnings allowed him to live comfortably for the rest of his natural life. However, after the publicity debacle with Pass Book, Fessenden was unable to maintain his winning streak. Although there is little known about the final decades of his life, he likely spent the entirety of those decades at his residence in New York City. He never married, fathered no children and had no contact with his family from Windham. On May 16, 1935, Wallace Clifton Fessenden passed away in New York City at the age of seventy-four.

12

CASE OF THE DISCOUNTED RAILROAD TICKET

In the 1880s, it was not uncommon for the Manchester & Lawrence Railroad to offer discounted tickets that could be purchased from the ticket agent at every station. A reduction of 25 percent or so in the price of a ticket was certainly an attractive offer for those who regularly traveled by train. Albert D. Swan of Lawrence was one such man to commute regularly by train. Late in the year of 1880, Swan arrived at Derry Depot intending to purchase a discounted ticket in order to travel back to Lawrence, Massachusetts. Shortly before Swan approached the ticket office window, the ticket agent had stepped out in order to help the baggage master load baggage onto a passenger train that was quickly approaching the station. Although this left the ticket office unattended, this was a common practice by the ticket agent because tickets could always be purchased aboard the train.

While the agent was helping to load the newly arrived train, Swan approached the depot's ticket office with the intention of purchasing a ticket that had been discounted from sixty-five cents to fifty cents. However, Swan noticed that the office was unattended and instead resolved to wait to purchase his ticket on the train. Although the train was scheduled to arrive at Derry Depot at precisely 11:31 a.m., it was running behind schedule; still, when the train arrived, the ticket agent was detained with other business. When the time came for the train to depart from Derry for Windham, Swan entered and handed the conductor the fifty cents for his one-way trip. To the annoyance of Swan, the conductor rejected his money and asked instead for the full fare of sixty-five cents. Swan steadfastly refused to pay the full price, as he could have purchased one at a lesser cost had the agent been diligent in his duties at the depot.

An altercation ensued, and Swan was ordered by the conductor to get off the train at Windham. Incidentally, W.S. Knox, a lawyer from Lawrence, had found himself in the same predicament as Swan and was also ordered off the train at Windham. At the station, Swan attempted to purchase a ticket from the Windham ticket agent, but he was refused a ticket for the rest of the trip to Lawrence. The conductor had spoken with the ticket agent in Windham and suggested that he not sell Swan the ticket, so Swan's money was returned to him; he was left stranded in Windham without any foreseeable means to get home. As a result, Swan was forced to go through considerable trouble in order to find someone to bring him to Lawrence; the cost of the trip by private means far exceeded the cost of even several full-price train tickets. Swan was evidently a man of principle and would rather go through unnecessary trouble and expense rather than be taken advantage of, by his own thinking, by the Manchester & Lawrence Railroad.

Upon arriving in Lawrence, Swan procured the services of a lawyer, E.T. Burley, in order to sue the railroad for $3,000 in damages. Although such an amount would seem to go far beyond any actual or punitive damages, Burley saw the potential for a large commission for himself and eagerly took on the case. Without one key piece of evidence, it would seem as if a strong case could be made for either side. Swan was unable to, by no fault of his own, purchase the discounted ticket at the depot. How could the railroad not honor the discounted price? However, in response to the suit, the railroad defended itself with a sign that had been posted in several places at the Derry stations. The sign specified that the fare from Derry to Lawrence was sixty-five cents. As for the discount, the sign stated that, according to the *Derry News*, "ticket sellers are authorized to make a deduction of 15 cents on local tickets when the tickets are procured at the ticket office."

In light of this evidence, the Massachusetts Supreme Court ruled that the sign clearly indicated Swan had not had a right to purchase a discounted ticket after boarding the train. As the depot had been open long before the arrival of the train, Swan had a reasonable chance to purchase one at the discounted rate. Although the ticket seller had left his post, the court realized that at many small stations, like those in Derry or Windham, the ticket agent would often take on additional duties if necessary. It would only hinder the

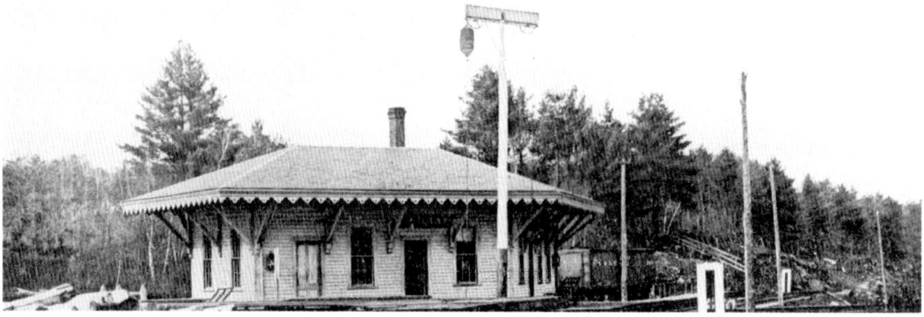

A photograph of Windham Depot as it would have appeared during the case. *From* History of Windham in New Hampshire (Rockingham County), 1719–1883.

service provided by the railroad if one of the few station employees was forced to remain behind a window for hours waiting for every single customer to purchase a ticket. Swan, who regularly traveled between Lawrence and New Hampshire, should have had the foresight to arrive at the station early enough to procure a ticket in the event that an unforeseen situation arose.

One of the other major points of the case was the refusal of the Windham ticket sales agent to sell to Swan a ticket to Lawrence. The court ruled that Swan had been rightfully rejected at the Windham station for refusing to pay the conductor the full fare. As the sign at the station had clearly stated a ticket could not be purchased from the conductor for a discount, there was no legal reason for Swan to object to paying the full price. Again, the Supreme Court ruled in favor of the defendant because the railroad company was not required to let Swan purchase a ticket to ride on the same train after being ejected by the conductor. On this point, the court decided that Swan was not just another passenger looking to begin a new transaction. Rather, he was attempting to renew the contract he had already broken. He could not at his own will arbitrarily break the transaction into two parts. As he had not paid for the trip from Derry to Windham, Swan had broken the contract and was, therefore, unable to continue the contract whenever he saw fit.

In the end, Swan was left with not only the cost of arranging his trip to Lawrence via a private carriage but also legal fees and the loss of many hours of his time spent tied up in the case. The case helped to provide added protection for the railroad industry from passengers who sought to take advantage of discount ticket sales. While many instances of case law were cited in the ruling for the case, *Swan v. Manchester and Lawrence Railroad* was significant in its ability to bring numerous rulings together to form a single ruling specifying the duties of the railroad in relation to the rights of passengers. In conclusion, the story of Albert Swan is one that highlights the nature of such frivolous lawsuits. Over the matter of fifteen cents, lawyers, judges and members of the court staff were left with many wasted hours, time that could have been spent on more pressing matters.

13

LAMSON'S FARM

William Stickney Lamson's dairy farm in Windham is but one example of the typical dairy farm in Windham at the turn of the twentieth century. Lamson was born in Newburyport, Massachusetts, in 1845. As a young man, he worked as a commercial artist and later served in the military for a brief period of time. Lamson married Mary-Anna Campbell of Windham sometime in the later years of the 1860s, and the couple had two sons, William-Abbot and Frank-Fitz. However, in the 1870s, Lamson saw the need for improving a new technology, the cash carrier; he filed for a patent for his improvements in 1879. The Lamson Cash Carrier Corporation was formed in 1882, following a patent being granted for a greatly improved cash railway system. The ancestor of the modern pneumatic cash delivery systems one may see at the drive-up window at a modern-day bank, this system was composed of sloping metal rails, on which a small container could slide to its destination. Many of the early models of this system were noisy, and the cash container was prone to falling off the rails. Although the cash railway promised a new, efficient way to transfer cash within a place of business, it would be years before it was perfected by William Stickney Lamson.

Lamson's patent describes several significant improvements that the inventor had made to the system, one of which was reducing the noise created as the container made its way around the track. One can imagine how irritated a shop clerk might get after spending all day listening to the sound of the metal track. Also, the newly patented system greatly reduced the likelihood that the container might slip off the rail after picking up some speed or making a particularly sharp turn. Other new features included an easier way to open and close the cash container, as well as making improvements with placing the container on and removing the container from the track.

When Lamson began to manufacture his product, his company quickly became successful, making him a wealthy man. By 1885, his company had installed nearly six hundred systems in stores across the nation. As the company grew, it bought out smaller rivals and eventually became the Lamson Company. Wishing to escape the city in the summers, Lamson purchased a farm in Windham in September 1892 for several thousand dollars. However, Lamson soon saw an opportunity to operate the farm as a business. Unlike the other farmers of Windham, Lamson had planned to open a farm store in Boston in order to sell the meat and dairy products produced at his farm. A period trade card advertises the "finest butter, eggs, milk, buttermilk, pork, lard, and sausages," all of which came from his Windham farm, located about forty miles from Boston. Everything was brought to the Boston store daily by train, ensuring only the freshest products were being sold to the customers in the city.

One of the workers at his farm was Ernest Hammond, who was born near the summit of Bauneg-Beg Mountain in North Berwick, Maine, in 1860. As a teenager, he gained experienced selling gardening and farming equipment with his father and brother. Within the span of several years, he saved both his father and younger brother from drowning on two separate occasions, earning him a reputation of being a courageous young man. When he was twenty-four years old, he decided to leave Maine to work on the flourishing farm of William Lamson. Lamson saw promise in the young man and offered him a position in the fruit department. However, Hammond was

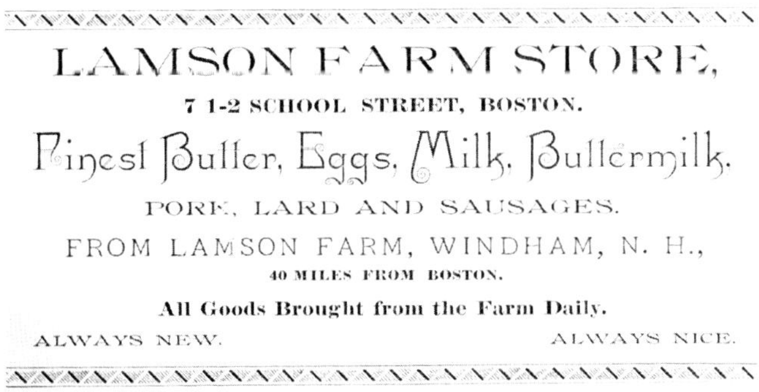

An 1890s trade card advertising Lamson's Farm Store in Boston, Massachusetts. *Author's collection.*

soon promoted to the manager of the Lamson Farm Store in Boston, as well as superintendent of the Windham farm.

On one of Hammond's regular business trips to Lowell, he was walking along the street when he saw a horse that had broken away from its hitching post heading in his direction. Living up to his reputation for being courageous, Hammond ran toward the horse and was able to wrap his arms around its head. Hammond was carried by the horse for some distance before his hold finally weakened and he was thrown into the street. The incident left him unconscious, and he was picked up and carried to the nearby Lowell Hospital. His condition was critical, with his face mangled, a bone broken and a severe injury to the back of his neck that almost cost him his life. Although he recovered from the broken bone and facial injuries, Hammond was plagued by neck problems for the rest of his life. His injuries naturally left him unable to continue his work for Lamson, and he left for Rhode Island soon after.

The creamery at Windham did not remain open long, closing after just a few years of operation. The farm was purchased by Traders & Mechanics Insurance Company; in 1896, the property was transferred to the National Angora Goat Raising Company. Although the property was no longer used for producing dairy, the dairy industry remained important in Windham until the 1950s. Refrigerated train cars, and later motor trucks, allowed local farmers to sell their milk and cream to larger operations, including H.P. Hood. However, eventually the large dairy companies began to purchase from only large, industrial-scale farms, and there was little business for the farmers of Windham.

14

A DAY AT GRANITE STATE GROVE

Before the heyday of the tourists traveling north to vacation at either Cobbett's Pond or Canobie Lake, one man had the vision to see Canobie Lake, then known as Policy Pond, as the perfect summer getaway. In 1850, a man whose name has been lost to history purchased a large lot of land along the Windham shore of Policy Pond in order to build Policy Pond Grove. The new business offered picturesque picnic groves where family and friends could gather and spend an afternoon eating lunch, shaded from the sun by the surrounding trees. Those looking to cool off during the hot days of the summer could take a swim in Policy Pond. For those not looking to get wet, or simply wanting to take a scenic ride around the lake, boats were docked along the shore, ready to be rowed for hours at a time.

Policy Pond Grove proved to be a great success, drawing large enough crowds to justify major improvements to the property in 1857. As some vacationers would not want to be bothered bringing a picnic lunch up from Massachusetts—or wherever they may have been traveling from—a small kitchen was opened to sell fresh meals to eager customers. Also, sailboats were added, giving those wanting to relax an alternative to rowing. When the improvements were completed, more and more people visited, increasing revenue more than ever. After the end of the Civil War, the business was successful enough to attract prospective buyers, and the operation was sold to William H. Smith in 1867.

Smith was even more ambitious with the business than the previous proprietor, adding the first bowling alley in Windham to the grove. He also built a large house and stables on the property. With more vacationers desiring to take a leisurely boat ride around Policy Pond, he also increased the number of boats for rent from twelve to fifteen. Smith had the business acumen and foresight to build Policy Pond Grove into a recreational destination that was unmatched by any similar venue in the area. With the business continually growing and providing Smith with a substantial income, Policy Pond Grove proved to be very attractive to Abel Dow. In 1877, Dow purchased the business.

Dow's purchase was at an opportune time, just before railways and street railways expanded to bring more vacationers to the area, stopping near Policy Pond. Shortly after purchasing the business, Dow renamed it to Dow's Grove, which later on seemed to be a wise choice, considering the name of the lake was soon after changed to Canobie Lake. However, the name Dow's Grove did not last long, as it was changed by Dow in 1896 to Granite State Grove.

As the lake became more and more accessible by the turn of the twentieth century, the recreational activities on the property had to be expanded, including the bowling alleys. Dow had also constructed a shooting gallery, where young men looking to impress a young lady or gain some bragging rights would take aim at the target with a small-caliber rifle. A roller skating rink was also constructed, which quickly became one of the most popular attractions at the grove. Finally, you could end your day at the dance hall, where the young and old could dance to live music from bands and individual singers.

Before the grove began to face competition from the opening of Canobie Lake Park on the opposing shore, the property also became a popular spot for outings. In 1901, the Court Nutfield chapter of the Foresters of America held their annual field day and picnic at Granite State Grove. Almost two hundred people were in attendance, mostly arriving by train, with a special train stopping at the grove just for the outing. Many of the guests were sure to take full advantage of the amusements at hand, patronizing all the recreational activities Dow had to offer. However, the big event of the day was a baseball game between the Salem Centers and the Derry Stars.

At 3:00 p.m. that day, the two rival teams faced off for the fourth time in that season. The Centers, having lost a game sixteen to zero the week before, were certainly hoping this game would be one of redemption for their team. Although the team might not have been highly regarded for its performance, there was one Salem player in particular who stood out that season. He was an old-timer named Wheeler who had a reputation for arguing every close

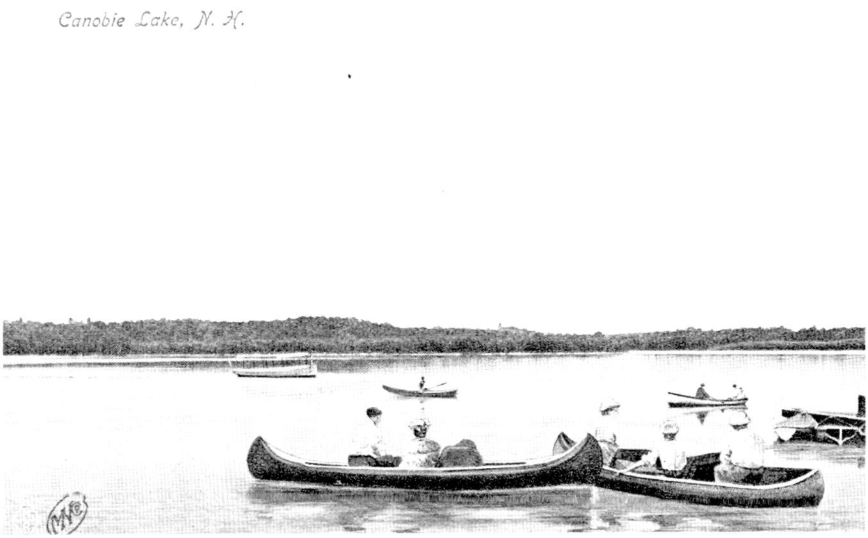

An early postcard showing Canobie Lake as seen by vacationers at Granite State Grove. *Author's collection.*

call; he was often successful and was responsible for garnering many points for the Centers.

Not having a regular baseball diamond to play on, the teams played rather close to the lake. However, there was one problem with this arrangement. Due to the baseball field's proximity to the water, the baseball found its way to the lake early on in the game. The soaking-wet ball made pitching more difficult, resulting in lousy pitches that made the game hard for not only the pitchers but also those up at bat. Despite the complications of a wet ball, Derry's pitcher, F. Sullivan, was able to strike out twelve batters, eleven of whom could not even make contact with the ball.

The performance of Salem's pitcher, Smith, was relatively lackluster, he having struck out only four of the Derry batters. Although the Centers played much better than they had the previous week, they still could not pull off a win, with the game's ending score being seven to four in favor of the Stars. The game had lasted for one hour and fifty-five minutes, much shorter than the average modern-day baseball game. This left the fans with ample time to enjoy the other activities offered at the grove.

One such activity was a game of tug of war, which took place between the Foresters and the Canado-Americaines. The Foresters were no match for their opponents, and the Canado-Americaines walked away victorious.

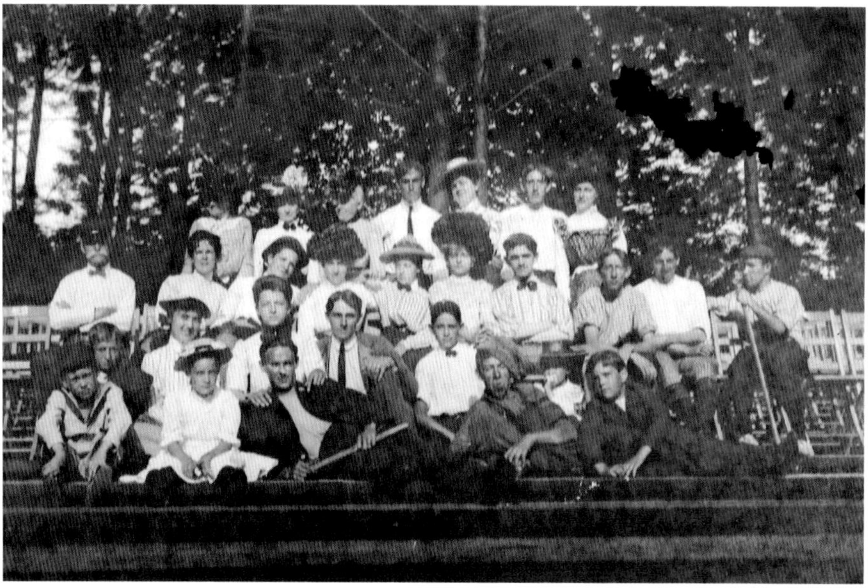

A group of summer vacationers on Canobie Lake, circa 1905. *Author's collection.*

Following this was a one-hundred-yard dash, which was won by an E. Smith, though there was no word on how long it took him to run the distance. For those looking for something a little less serious than the distance sprint, a sack race and a three-legged race were held. The winners of those races were C. Sling and the team of J. Gibeau and C. Sling, respectively. As no track and field event would be complete without some form of a long jump, one was held, and W. Clark took first prize.

With an open lake to use, it would only make sense that there would also be competitive events taking place on the water. The first of these was a boat race, which was won by David DeVarney. There was also a swimming contest that was won by H. Low. Prizes were awarded to the winners, but there is no record of what the prizes were. After a long, hot summer day, a day spent at the lake was likely a prize itself; it is doubtful any of the contestants truly cared about the prizes awarded that day.

It was fortunate the outdoor activities took place earlier in the day when the weather could not have been better, as it began to downpour soon after the day's games concluded. This drove the crowds to the indoor amusements, especially the skating rink and the dance hall. The music at the dance hall for the night was provided by Madden's orchestra from Derry. The group owed its name to J.W. Madden of Manchester, who was the promoter. When the special train arrived at Granite State Grove to bring the crowd back to Derry at 11:30 p.m., everyone departed knowing a summer day could have been spent in no better way.

However, there would not be many more summer days spent leisurely at the grove. For the next several years, Granite State Grove had a series of setbacks that eventually forced it to close indefinitely. First, with the opening of Canobie Lake Park nearby in 1903, the original attraction on the lake began to lose customers. Also, in 1903, swimming in Canobic Lake was banned, leaving the grove without one of its most popular recreational activities. Finally, on July 21, 1909, came the most devastating setback yet for the business. On that day, a fire began around noon in the skating rink. The fire spread quickly throughout the other buildings on the property and many of the trees in the grove also burned. Although the fire was eventually put out, there was an estimated $15,000 of damages. Unfortunately for Dow, he was unable to collect any insurance money on the property, and Granite State Grove never reopened.

15

EDWARD FRANCIS SEARLES

They say—what say they? Let them say.

Above is the personal motto of Edward Francis Searles, a man who went from rags to riches, from working in mills to building lavish castle estates. He was born on the Fourth of July in 1841 in Methuen, Massachusetts, to parents Jessie Gould Searles and Sarah Littlefield Searles. His father, a farmer and superintendent at a local cotton mill, passed away when Searles was only two years old. The family could not survive long on any assets that Sarah might have had, so she was forced to send Edward and his brother, Andrew, to work in the cotton mill as soon as they were old enough.

With money from selling part of the family farm and from Edward working in local cow pastures, as well as at the mill, Sarah was able to pay for her son to take piano lessons in Lawrence, Massachusetts. Edward developed an interest in the piano and went on to study organ music in Boston, later teaching piano and organ. When household chores became too much for Sarah, she decided to find a young girl to help with housekeeping. Not having money to pay standard wages to an interested young lady, she opted to provide free room and board as partial payment for the services.

In 1858, an Irish girl, Catherine Linehan, arrived at the Searles home to assist with the domestic chores. Andrew and Edward both immediately became very fond of her, but both sons left home soon after—Edward leaving to teach music in Maine and Andrew enlisting to fight for the Union in the Civil War. With Andrew still off serving his country, Edward came home to Methuen after spending two years teaching. Catherine was still boarding at

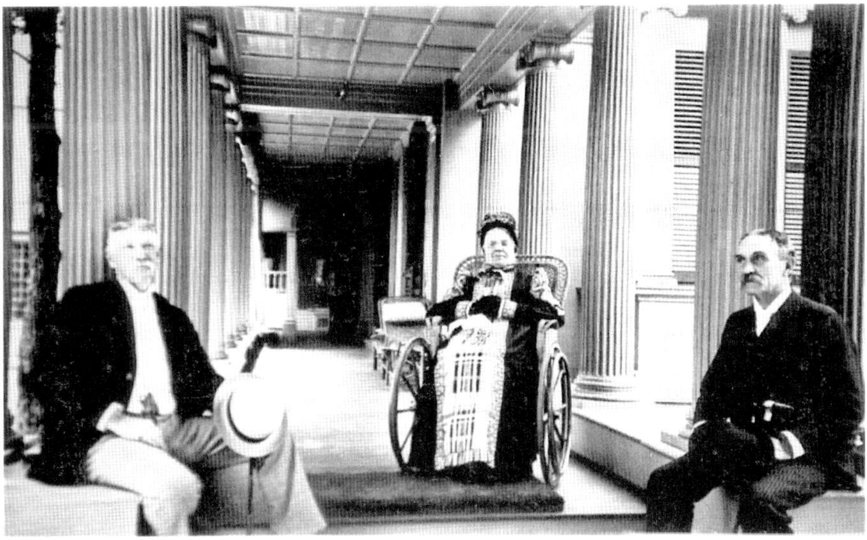

Edward Searles (left) with his elderly mother (center). *City of Methuen Archives.*

the family home, and Edward now found her even more beautiful than she was when he left. Eventually, Catherine and Edward became engaged, but the relationship fell apart with the conclusion of the Civil War.

By the end of the war, Andrew had attained the rank of major and arrived back home in Methuen wearing his decorated uniform proudly. Soon after the arrival of Andrew, Catherine broke her engagement with Edward. Although there is no known reason for this, one would likely be correct to say the young major was more appealing to Catherine than the piano teacher. Andrew and Catherine were married in New York City in 1867.

By this time, Edward had left home in search of employment, eventually securing a job with Paul and Co., an interior design firm in Boston. It was under the employment of the firm that Edward became interested in architecture and interior design, an interest that would stay with him for the rest of his life. After spending several years in Boston, Edward quit his job to spend six years traveling Europe with the money he had been able to save.

Upon his return from Europe, Edward obtained employment with another interior design firm, Herter Brothers, in New York. Herter Brothers served clients across the country, including some of the richest and most prominent people in the nation. By 1881, Edward had been able to accumulate a small fortune under the employment of the firm. However, he soon fell ill with rheumatic fever, forcing him to leave his job. He was advised by friends to leave for the milder, dryer climates of the western states, possibly California. As fate would have it, his trip west would change his life in a way he could have never imagined.

Before leaving Herter Brothers, Searles had agreed to visit some of the California mansions the firm had furnished, should he have the chance. However, there was one home in particular Searles was asked to visit. This was the palatial estate of railroad magnate Mark Hopkins located in the Nob Hill district of San Francisco. At the time of Searles's visit, Mark Hopkins was recently deceased, and the home was occupied by only his widow and domestic workers. Searles was granted entry to the estate upon furnishing the calling card of a friend.

Hopkins had followed the miners westward during the gold rush of 1849, opening a hardware store with C.P. Huntington. Although they started small, selling pans to gold miners, the partners continued to invest their profits in gold mines and land, eventually building a fortune. They used this fortune to build the Central Pacific Railroad with three other men. In 1854, Hopkins returned to the East, going to Great Barrington, Massachusetts, to marry his cousin, Mary Frances Sherwood. When Hopkins died in 1878, his widow was the beneficiary of his $31.7 million fortune—equivalent to about three quarters of a billion dollars in 2016.

The couple's only child was an adopted son, Timothy Nolan. It was Timothy Nolan Hopkins himself who delivered a dinner invitation to Searles following his visit to the home of his mother. Upon concluding his business with Hopkins, Searles left with an order for a grand piano for the Nob Hill home. There was also an agreement to consider some work to be done at the widow's hometown of Great Barrington. She had planned to spend about $900,000, a very substantial sum for the period, to build "Kellogg Terrace." Hopkins's taste for excellence and Searles's interest in design necessitated a trip to Europe to obtain the materials needed to complete the project.

As Hopkins continued to meet with Searles for the duration of the project, the two fell in love, despite Hopkins being twenty-two years older than Searles. Although Hopkins was certainly attracted to Searles, Searles was much more interested in her money. When it came time for marriage, Searles even admitted that money was one of the motives behind his decision to marry Hopkins, but he always maintained that he truly loved her. When Hopkins proposed to Searles in 1883, an uncommon occurrence for the period, he responded by asking her for one year to consider the proposal. When the one year was up, he proposed to her, but she refused. It would be another three years before the couple eventually married in 1887.

Before the couple was married, a prenuptial agreement was drawn up to protect Hopkins from any interest Searles might have had in her fortune. However, Searles was given a building on Broadway in New York City, as well as a large block of stock in the *New York Globe* as gifts from his fiancée. Also, Searles received half of the estate of Hopkins on his wedding day, an arrangement Searles claimed to have no prior knowledge of. The new bride made out a will soon after their marriage that bequeathed $10,000 to a favorite employee of hers, with the rest of her estate being divided equally between Searles and Timothy.

Despite Hopkins's vast wealth, the wedding was a simple affair that took place in Trinity Chapel in New York City, where Dr. William H. Platt married the couple. The early morning wedding was then followed by breakfast at Delmonico's restaurant with Platt. Soon after they were married, the couple left for a six-month tour of Europe for their honeymoon. Hopkins and Searles seemed to desperately want company, and as they did not likely have too many friends, Platt's family, including his wife and daughter, joined the newlywed couple on their trip. Although Edward had a strong distaste for publicity, the wedding made news all over the country, particularly in California.

Little is known about their life as a married couple after they returned to America. Neither Searles nor his wife received many visitors at their lavish estates, and few people ever visited their "Pine Lodge" estate in Methuen, Massachusetts, where the couple resided much of the time. It is recorded that Mary routinely worshipped at St. Thomas's Episcopal Church but had little contact with any of the other parishioners. However, she made generous donations to the church on a couple of occasions, which included outfitting the church with new carpets. As a typical millionaire, she would be driven to church in a lavish carriage, which attracted the attention of many residents of Methuen and nearby Lawrence. Unfortunately, for those hoping to catch a glimpse of one of the country's richest women, she would always shield her face with a parasol when traveling in her carriage.

Although some of her reluctance to be seen in public may be attributed to her and her husband's distaste for publicity of any kind, she was also known to be sensitive to what she saw as her physical imperfections. She was also a rather unhealthy woman, dying just four years after she was married. The winter before her passing, she had suffered from a flu-like illness, from which she was never able to fully recover. While residing in Great Barrington the following year, Mary was overcome with another illness, which a doctor pronounced as terminal. She was brought to Methuen to spend the last summer of her life.

Mary Hopkins-Searles passed away on Friday, July 25, 1891, at four o'clock in the morning. Her death was determined to be the result of a lethal combination of heart disease and edema. The funeral was held four days later, with everything being done as secretly as possible. Prior to her funeral, the Methuen estate was guarded by plainclothes detectives who were hired to prevent newspaper reporters from entering. When the private service was held, only about fifty people were invited. Reverend Charles F. Sweet of St. Thomas's Episcopal Church was chosen to conduct the service.

With prominent Methuen citizens and several members of the Hopkins family in attendance, the service was unusual in that there were absolutely no flowers. The forty-minute service included organ music, perhaps to satisfy Searles's lasting love for the instrument. At the conclusion of the service, the body of the deceased was brought to a tomb on Lawrence Street in Methuen. Although the tomb was incomplete when Mrs. Searles passed away, workmen worked speedily on the Sunday after her death to finish it. The completed tomb was twenty by twenty-five feet and about twenty-five feet high. There was room for not only the body of Mrs. Searles but also five other additional bodies.

When her will was filed in the Salem, Massachusetts probate court by Mr. Searles, a sensation was caused when the public heard the latest copy of Hopkins's will left Timothy Hopkins nothing—not a single cent. At the time, Hopkins was traveling back to America from Japan and could not be reached concerning the filing. Most of the media and the public correctly assumed that he would contest the will. After a long, bitter fight, the will was upheld in Searles's favor, but Hopkins did not give up and filed an appeal with the state Supreme Court. This appeal was withdrawn by Hopkins when Searles settled with him for $3 million.

As the public opinion generally sided with Hopkins, the court battles left Searles with even more of a distaste for publicity, and he withdrew from public life more so than ever. In the decade following the settlement of his late wife's estate, Searles spent time working on his several estates, including Stillwater Manor in Salem, New Hampshire. Shortly after the turn of the century, Searles purchased land in Windham, which overlooked Cobbett's Pond, with the intention to build an estate there. On the estate, he worked with architect Henry Vaughn to build a scale replica of the historic Stanton-Harcourt castle; the completed project only slightly resembled the original castle.

When construction began on the castle in 1905, it was intended that it be built on Jenny's Hill so that it could not be looked down upon by the Nevins and the Tenneys of Methuen, of whom Searles was very jealous. However, the location proved to be unsuitable for the project, and the building that was being constructed was dismantled and moved to a nearby hill.

Searles spared no expense in building his Windham estate, even opening a quarry in Pelham, specifically for the purpose of supplying much of the granite that was needed for the project. The red sandstone trim on the castle was shipped in from Ohio. With Searles's background in interior design, the interior of the castle was nothing less than magnificent. To enter the main reception room from the opening foyer, one would pass through doors from Windsor Castle. Upon entering, one would be immediately drawn to an elaborate fireplace from the home of Napoleon Bonaparte himself; this was acquired by Searles for the princely sum of $50,000. Hundreds of thousands of dollars were spent completing the other rooms of the castle, using only the highest-quality materials available.

The Windham estate was enclosed on three sides by fieldstone walls, with the fourth side being enclosed by a wire fence. During Searles's stay at the estate, there was an attendant stationed at each entrance, readily awaiting the arrival of Searles in his Pierce Arrow.

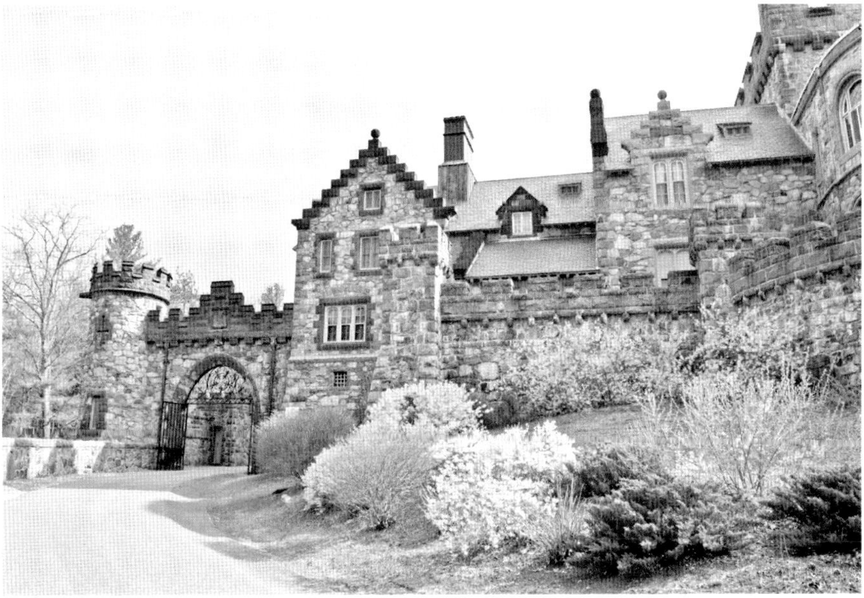

The front of Searles Castle as seen from the path leading to the iron-gated entryway. *Mark Cantrell.*

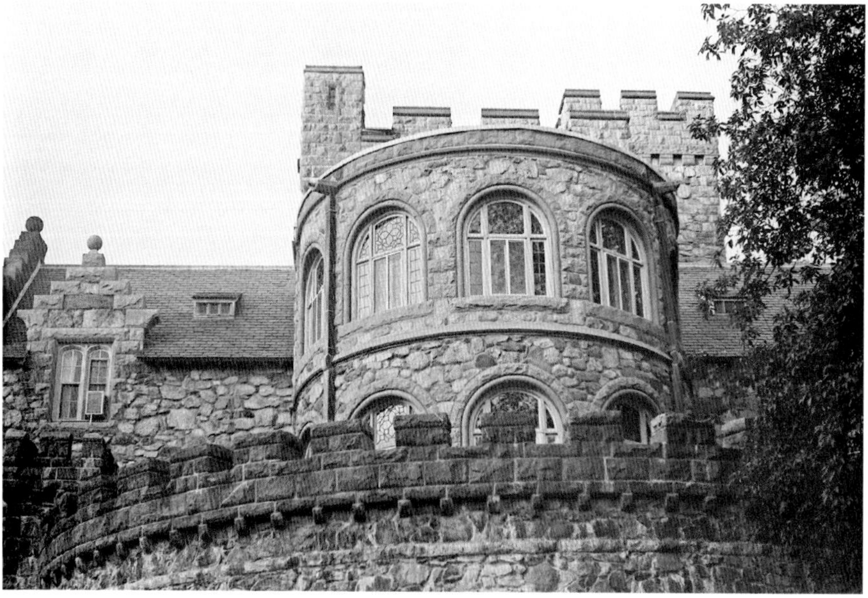

A wall built around the castle shielded the first floor from the prying eyes of the curious and gave the estate an authentic medieval appearance. *Mark Cantrell.*

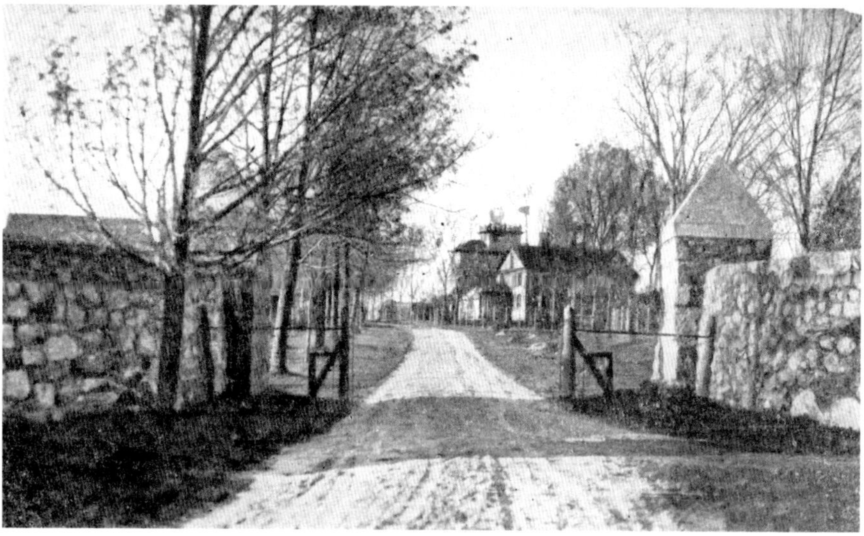

The gated entrance to Searles's estate is where attendants would have waited for his arrival. *Author's collection.*

Searles, who was accustomed to using his wealth to purchase whatever he wanted, encountered several problems in Windham. First, he greatly desired to purchase a piece of land located between Range Road and the original Indian Rock Road. However, the owner, Dan Roy, would not sell. Searles responded by building a wall around one side of the desired property and purchasing property that abutted the other three sides. Roy never gave in, leaving Searles to move on to other endeavors.

A second issue arose when Searles had acquired land, which surrounded School House No. 1. As it was important for Searles to have control of the entire property, he offered the town a new schoolhouse and the land on which it would be built in exchange for the old schoolhouse. This time, Searles met little resistance and built the town a $40,000 Tudor-style schoolhouse, with the provision that it could be used only for educational or religious purposes.

Searles's accumulation of New Hampshire property proved to be in vain, for he was taxed in 1913 on his cash assets, which represented much of his fortune. As the value of Searles's estate dwarfed that of the entire population of Windham, the tax rate significantly dropped to about $0.55 per $1,000.00. The town also had to deal with a new problem it had not previously run into: what would the tax windfall be used for?

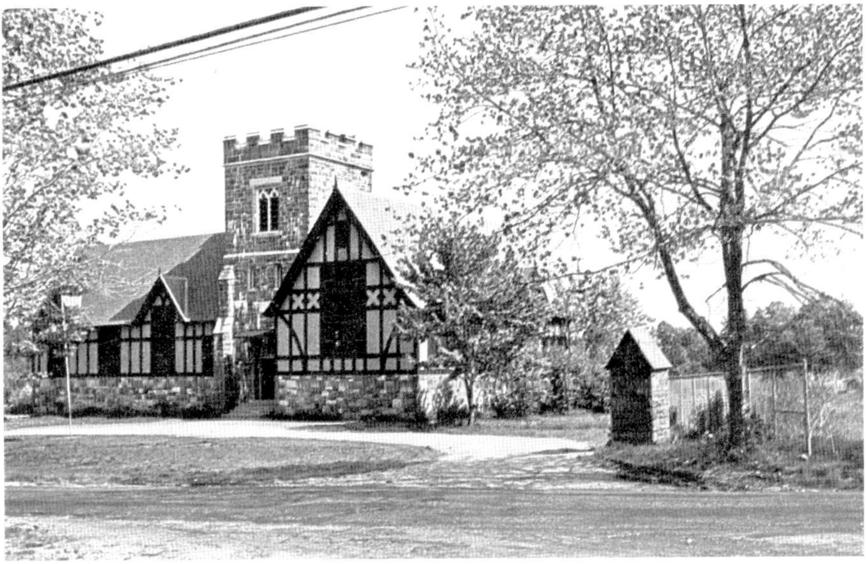

The school Searles built for the town in exchange for Schoolhouse No. 1. *Author's collection.*

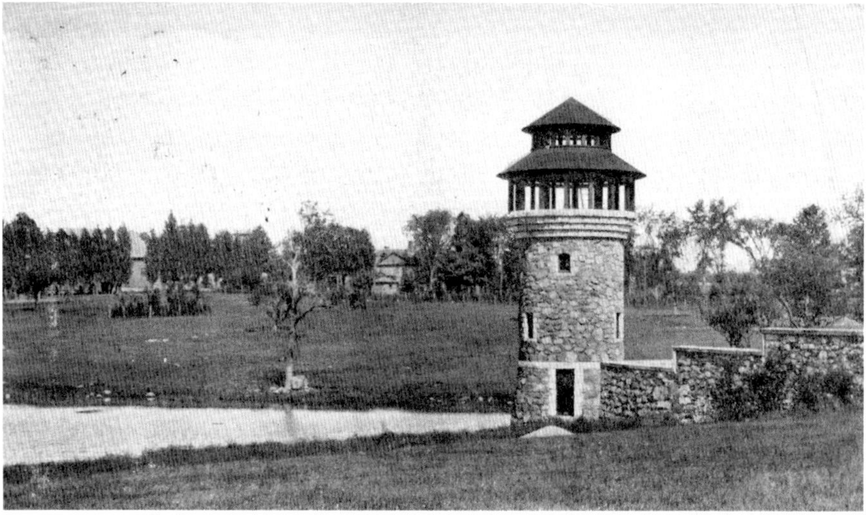

A circa 1920 postcard showing one of the large stone towers constructed on the Searles estate. *Author's collection.*

The town's selectmen decided and the voters agreed that the money would be best put to use for roadwork. To complete the work, a steamroller and stone crusher were purchased with the intention of working near Windham Depot and on Kendall Pond Road. However, the construction workers were more focused on play than work and would take time off to play a game of baseball whenever they felt the urge to. Also, Searles left town in 1914 because of the taxes, leaving Windham without the tax revenue to finish the project. After leaving town, Searles purchased Rockingham Park in Salem.

Searles died at the age of seventy-nine on August 6, 1920, at his estate in Methuen. His funeral was held the following Tuesday, with 150 guests in attendance, including relatives and employees. Keeping with Searles's distaste for publicity, no newspaper reporters were allowed admittance to the services, which were held in the great hall of Pine Lodge. The body of Searles remained hidden from view in a closed casket, denying guests a final glimpse of the eccentric millionaire. Although there were later rumors of murder by poisoning, these were dispelled when his tomb was opened and an autopsy was performed.

16

COBBETT'S POND

The history of Cobbett's Pond begins with the man whose name the pond eventually came to bear, Reverend Thomas Cobbet. Cobbet received the pond in a land grant in 1663. However, he never actually lived on the land, and neither did any other Europeans until 1719. Much of Cobbett's Pond's early history involves the Native Americans of the Penacook tribe who lived in the area. The pond was a favorite fishing spot of the Native Americans, and they would also grow their crops in the vicinity of the pond. When it was time to grind the grain, they could make a trip by canoeing across, or walking around, the pond to a large boulder near the north side. Small indentations on the boulder are evidence of its use as a mortar for grinding grains with a hand-fashioned stone pestle. Aside from the boulder, many arrowheads have been found around the pond, suggesting it was a popular spot for the Native Americans.

One of the earliest references made to the pond referred to the body of water as Draw Pond. Why this name was chosen has been lost to history. The name Cobbett's, or some variation of it, was used to describe the pond as early as the first half of the eighteenth century. Before the name Cobbett's was used almost exclusively for the pond in the late nineteenth century, many variations were used. These include Cabot's, Corbett's and Cobbet's; the pond was also referred to as Cabbage Pond at one time, but it is up to the reader to decide how one might have derived that name from any of the other spellings.

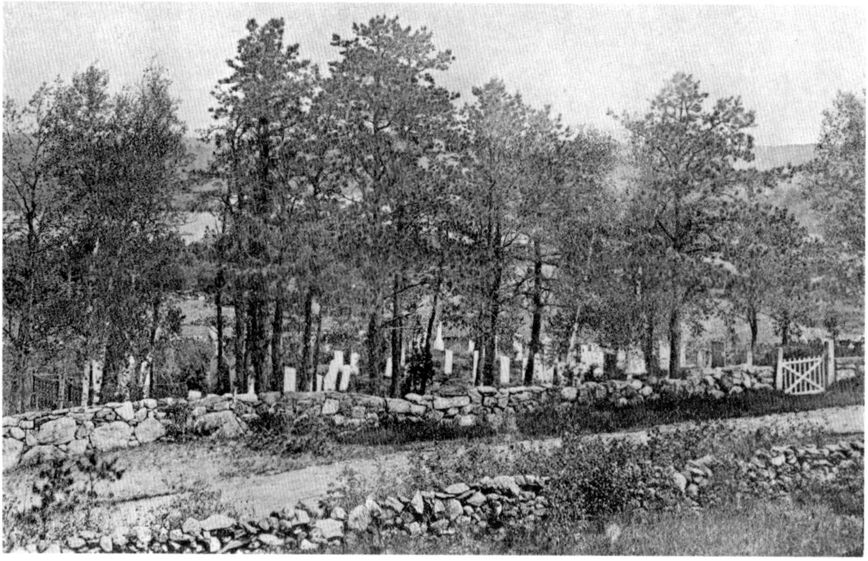

An 1883 photograph of the Cemetery on the Hill, where many of the early settlers were buried. *From* History of Windham in New Hampshire (Rockingham County), 1719–1883.

The first settlement in Windham was located near the shores of Cobbett's Pond; a home was built on Copp's Hill by John Waddell around 1720. Windham's early settlers were likely attracted to the pond by its untouched, picturesque setting. Not only did some of the settlers build their homes overlooking the pond, but one of the town's first cemeteries was also laid out on the east shore of the pond, giving the deceased a permanent place overlooking the body of water.

In 1728, a group of fourteen Londonderry farmers received grants for land on the south and east sides of Cobbett's Pond in order to settle a dispute over the tracts of land they had originally received. The landholders argued that when their land, in what is now Derry, was laid out, each was not given a fair share. Eventually, the proprietors settled by offering the men a total of 594 acres of land, which reached from Cobbett's Pond to Canobie Lake. These farms were some of the most prosperous in town for over a century.

When the town hall and Presbyterian Church were built at the town center, some of those who lived along the shore of Cobbett's Pond routinely traveled there via rowboat. Whether it be attending church service on Sunday or for other business, a trip by boat would have certainly been quicker and more efficient than making the trip on foot or by horse. However, one such trip proved to be fatal on one particular occasion. On November 2, 1834,

Reverend Jacob Abbott and John Dinsmoor, along with each of their two sons, decided to cross the pond by boat in order to attend church. Out of precaution, they decided two trips should be made for the group so as to not overload the boat.

However, when they were returning from church service, the decision was made that such a precaution was not necessary; all six should return home in the same boat. The added weight only worsened the condition of the boat that was already prone to leak. It began to take on water at a much greater rate than it did that morning, and the boat capsized before the group could make it to shore. Fortunately for the young men, they were able swimmers and swam to shore, although one did have some difficulty. Ebenezer Abbott went down with the boat three times before he was able to save himself. On the third time down, his finger became caught in the boat's chain, which made it possible for him to grab the chain and pull himself up. It is recorded that he kept that chain for the rest of his life. Their fathers were not so fortunate; Reverend Abbott and Dinsmoor both drowned.

Farmers whose pastureland was located along the shores of the pond saw the location as advantageous due to the easy access their animals had to fresh water. Not only was the crisp, clean pond a source of water for farm animals, but it also had plenty of uses for those living near the pond. If water was needed for cooking purposes or any other household chore, it would have been convenient to take a short stroll down to Cobbett's Pond and fill a bucket or two with water. When winter came along, the pond proved to be a valuable source of ice, which was used for storing perishable foodstuffs. The pond was also a prime fishing spot, undoubtedly providing many families with food. These were among the many reasons why Cobbett's Pond became so valuable to the early inhabitants of Windham. However, by the turn of the nineteenth century, the reasons behind the allure of the pond began to shift.

As cities grew around the mills of Massachusetts, more and more people wished to escape the hot, crowded cities during the summer months. The appeal of a cool, clean lake or pond would have been almost irresistible. Summer vacationers had already been visiting nearby Canobie Lake for decades, so it was only natural that Cobbett's Pond would also become a summer destination. In 1883, the Horne family of Lowell, Massachusetts, became the first people to purchase land on Cobbett's Pond for the purpose of spending summers there. For the first several years, the family stayed in a tent near the shore, but eventually a cottage was built.

The first cottage on the pond was built by Frank Ayer in 1886. It was built on land owned by G.W. Noyes. Ayers led a group of men from Nashua, who

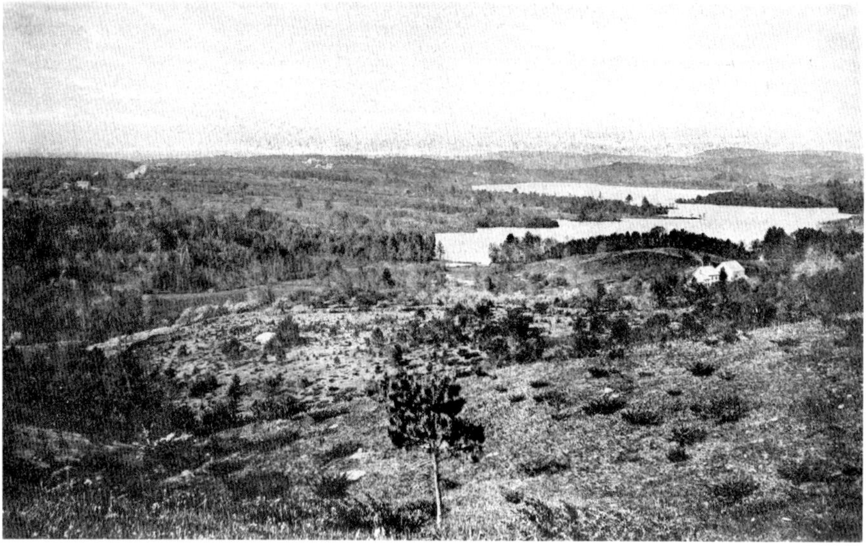

This view of Cobbett's Pond from the north shore shows how the shoreline looked in 1883, before any summer cottages were constructed. *From* History of Windham in New Hampshire (Rockingham County), 1719–1883.

desired to use the cottage as a summer getaway. By the late 1890s, the Ayer cottage was no longer alone on the pond, as many cottages were constructed along the shores of the pond. In 1894, Albert Simpson constructed a public resort named Sycamore Grove at the south end of the pond. Although not an amusement attraction like its competitor, Granite State Grove, the operation did attract many picnickers. The business and land were sold to Julia Baker shortly after the turn of the twentieth century; incidentally, she was one of the first Windham residents to own a motor car.

In 1895, William Harris saw a different type of seasonal potential in the pond, and he began constructing cottages on the north shore. This summer colony became one of the fastest-growing cottage colonies on the pond at the time. However, summer vacationers seeking to reach their summer cottage or just spend a day at the pond were met with inadequate transportation. As cars were still not commonplace, many were forced to take a train, usually to Canobie Lake Station. From here, some would either walk or be met by friends who would take them by wagon or carriage to the pond. One enterprising Salem man by the name of E.J. Nickerson opened a business offering to pick up vacationers at the station and bring them to Cobbett's Pond.

Those with an entrepreneurial sense, such as Charles Alexander and Charles Dow, saw the demand for cottages as the foundation for a successful real estate development enterprise. In 1903, Dow and Alexander bought one mile of waterfront land, which was then subdivided into sixty-six fifty-foot lots. The development necessitated building a horseshoe-shaped road leading from Range Road, which ran parallel to the pond, to each of the lots. One of the original stipulations in the land deeds was that each new owner would maintain his own section of the road. After the first year of marketing the lots, only six had been sold and just one cottage had been built. Some lots took nearly two decades to sell. In 1918, Alexander sold a lot to Karl Norris, who then resold it in 1924 to the author's paternal great-grandfather Erich Obst. Although the lot may have been small, the price could not have been beat—Obst paid one dollar. A boathouse and cottage were eventually erected on the site, and the Obst family spent many wonderful summers at Cobbett's Pond for several decades.

The popularity of the pond began to increase, and the lots eventually began to sell as more and more cottages were built. By 1912, there were seventy cottages on Cobbett's Pond. Many of these cottages had a rowboat or canoe, as no summer on the pond could be complete without a day spent fishing or simply enjoying being out on the water. As early as the first decade of the twentieth century, there was at least one motorboat on the pond, an unusual sight for those who had never seen the then

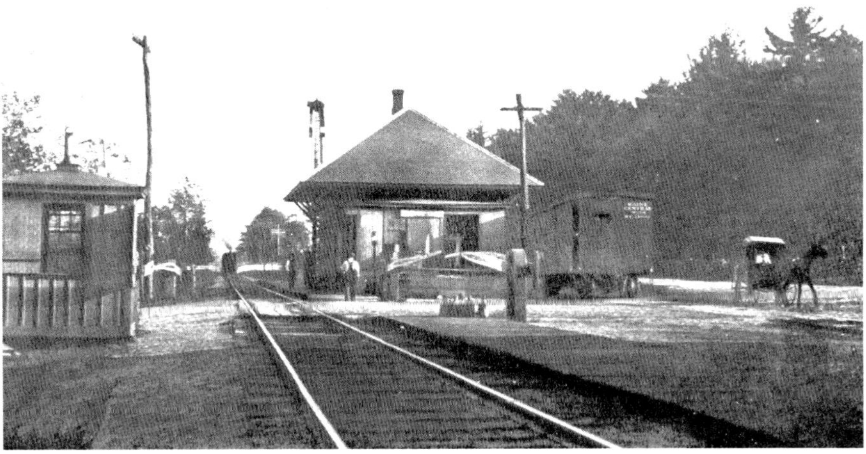

Canobie Lake Station, circa 1910. During the summer months, the trains stopping at the station would be filled with passengers on their way to Cobbett's Pond. *Author's collection.*

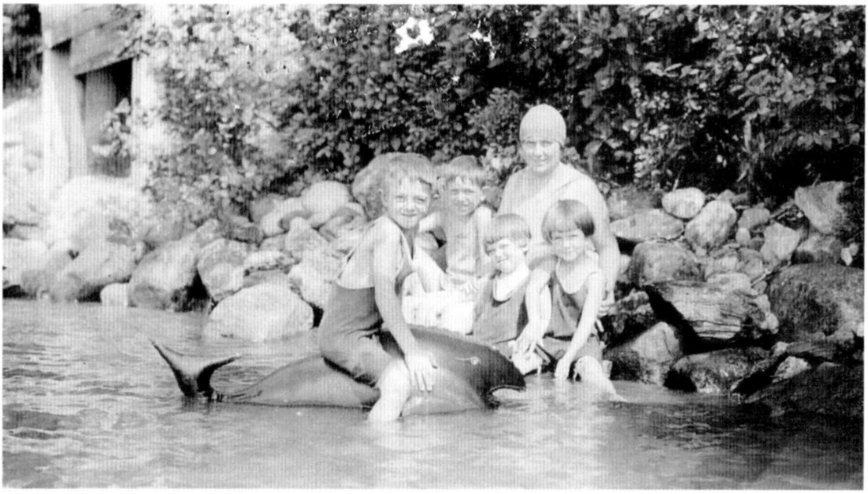

Helen Obst and her four children enjoying a summer day at Cobbett's Pond in the early 1930s. *Author's collection.*

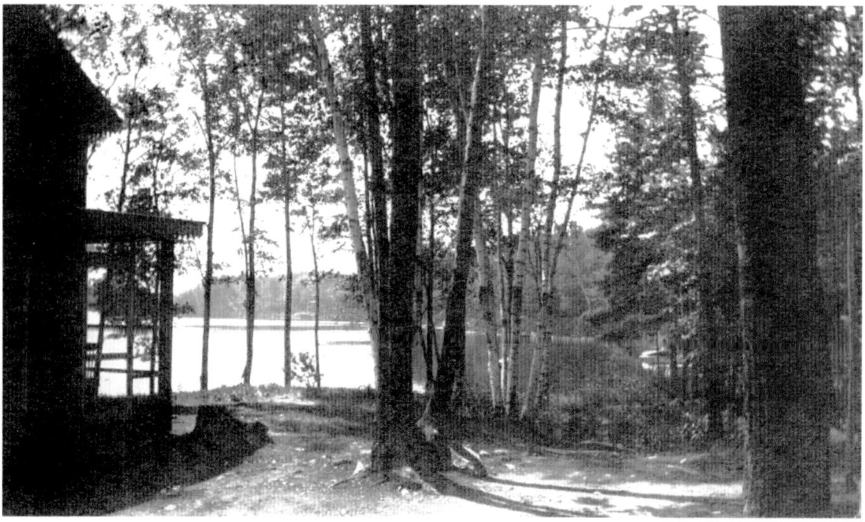

A circa 1910 view of Cobbett's Pond from the back porch of Shady Shore Cottage. The cottage would have been one of many rented to summer vacationers. *Author's collection.*

modern technology. In 1911, Henry Newhall brought his four-horsepower motorboat to his summer cottage on the pond. Many of his neighbors were understandably jealous.

As decades passed and the popularity of Cobbett's Pond only grew, other real estate speculators decided to take advantage of the high demand for lots. In 1929, a syndicate named Lake Shore Development Trust was formed to purchase sixty acres of land near the pond. Only looking to turn a profit, the land was subdivided into 975 lots, plus a community beach and a playground. The lots were around twenty by one hundred feet, which were not suitable for building an average-size summer cottage. However, those who were looking to build a small shack or tent would have found their needs perfectly met by these new lots. Each of the waterfront lots sold for fifty dollars, and the back lots sold for just twenty dollars. There was a catch though; each buyer had to pay the property owners an additional fifty dollars to record the deed.

This venture was not very successful due to a combination of two major drawbacks. First, there were no properly built roads to the lots. It was the responsibility of the purchasers to build the road. Second, many of the lots

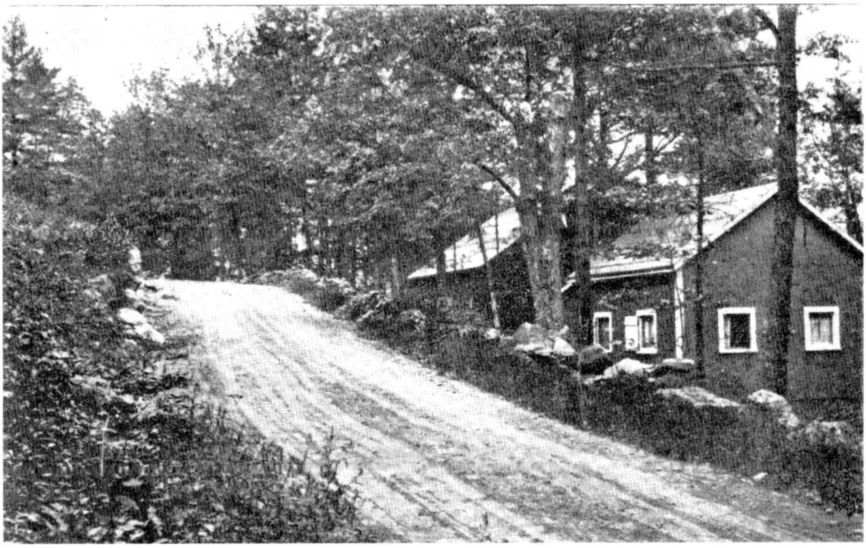

Butler's camps along the shore of Cobbett's Pond. The camps were one of several small rental cottage "colonies" on the pond. *Author's collection.*

were much too far from the water. Although there was a community beach, many prospective buyers desired their own water frontage or, at least, a relatively clear view of the pond. When the owners were left paying taxes on properties that were seemingly unsalable, they came up with an unusual strategy to liquidate the remaining lots.

Rather than sell lots, they would give them away. Through a promotional deal with local grocery stores, one of the back lots would be given away with the purchase of either five pounds of tea or a single pound of coffee; to take ownership of the lot, there was still a fifty-dollar recording fee. This scheme was rather successful, and twenty cottages had been built on the lots by 1934. When the same property owners failed to sell some of their lots around a pond in Pelham, they used the same scheme, which was also rather successful. Giving away the lots may have also helped to sell other lots. When someone took ownership of a lot and wanted to build on it, they would've been forced to purchase at least a few surrounding lots in order to have a large enough parcel.

Not everyone who desired to spend a summer day at Cobbett's Pond had the luxury of owning a cottage or even an unimproved lot. For locals and vacationers alike, there were several beaches around the pond that were open to the public. Beaches, including Hadley's and Bella Vista, were prime spots for both swimming and picnicking. Those who were looking for a little excitement could pay a quarter for a boat ride on one of the boats of the Dunkley brothers. As late as the middle of the twentieth century, boats were still somewhat of a novelty, and a ride on a Gar Wood or a Christ Craft was certainly an event not easily forgotten.

The beaches also offered summer refreshments, such as hot dogs and ice cream. At Dunkan's Beach, a pavilion was eventually constructed that grew to include a jukebox, pinball machines and a gift shop. Bud's Corner operated as a snack stand near the south shore of the pond and sold a variety of summer refreshments, from ice cream to fried clams. Still, swimming was the biggest attraction at the beaches. As the number of swimmers grew, there became a need to ensure the safety of the public. Although many beaches had lifeguards, there was not a town ordinance requiring them until the early 1970s. The same ordinance also required that the lifeguard have access to a telephone as well as the appropriate emergency equipment. However, many of the beach owners were not so keen on the new regulations. They argued that on some days, many people came to picnic rather than swim, and hiring a lifeguard would have been an extraneous expense; there were also some days when the number of people swimming would not have warranted a lifeguard.

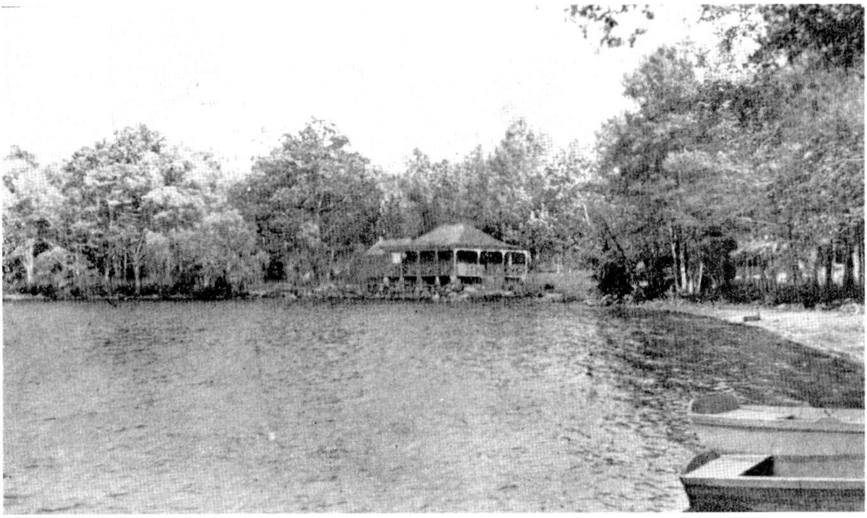

The pavilion on Cobbett's Pond; one of the earliest recreational businesses to operate on the pond. *Author's collection.*

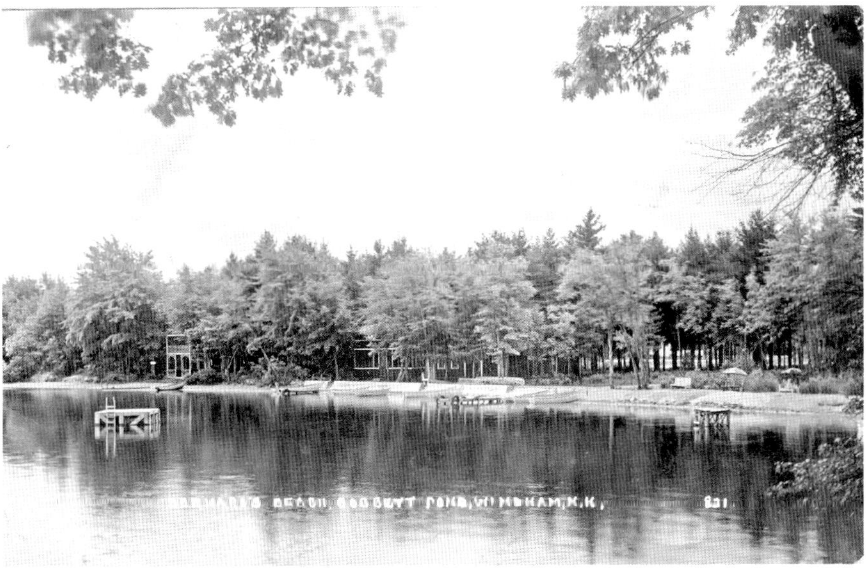

Bernard's Beach on Cobbett's Pond as it appeared in 1933. *Author's collection.*

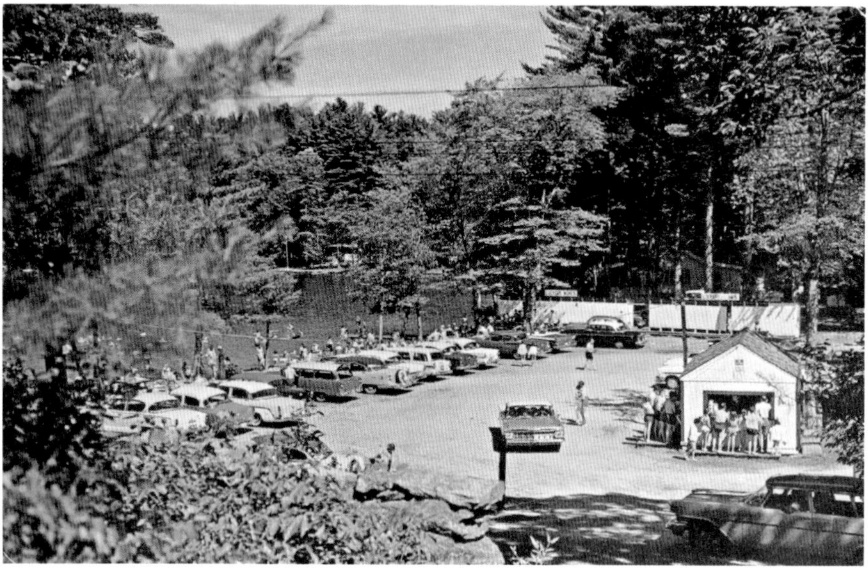

A mid-twentieth-century postcard view of Hadley's Beach on the south shore of Cobbett's Pond. The beach now serves as Windham's town beach. *Author's collection.*

The beaches did not last long. Within the next decade, many of the beaches closed, and access to Cobbett's Pond by nonresidents was severely limited. It also became increasingly hard for summer vacationers to find a rental property along the pond, as many homes were privately owned. What was once a thriving tourist destination gave way to a relatively densely populated, for Windham, residential area. As of this writing, two of the original beaches still exist on the pond. One is Community Beach, which is still privately owned by surrounding property owners. The other is the former location of Hadley's Beach, which now serves as a beach open to only town residents. Despite all the changes, it is still possible for Windham residents to spend a day fishing or swimming in Cobbett's Pond, just as the vacationers of one hundred years ago did.

17

CHICK AUSTIN'S PLAYHOUSE

Shortly after Everett "Chick" Austin was gifted the eighteenth-century home of Lieutenant Joseph Smith in Windham as a wedding gift from his mother, he delighted the residents of the town with a magic show. Although Austin's performance in the town hall would have certainly paled in comparison to the feats of Houdini and history's other great magicians, his charisma and talent for performing were able to hold the audience mesmerized for over two hours. This would not be the last time he was responsible for captivating the audiences of Windham and the surrounding locales.

Arthur Everett Austin Jr. was born on December 18, 1900, in Brookline, Massachusetts, to parents Dr. Arthur Everett Austin and Laura Etnier Austin. As his birthday was just a week shy of Christmas, Everett, as he was known to his family, grew up believing that the tinsel and other ornamental decorations of the season were for the celebration of his birthday rather than the holiday.

Because his mother was wealthy, young Everett was fortunate to have the opportunity to spend his childhood exploring Europe, although it appears this worldliness did not help him in his studies. His lackluster academic abilities made his acceptance to Harvard somewhat shocking. However, the school soon came to the realization that he was not cut from the same intellectual cloth as his classmates, and he was asked to leave.

Fortunately for Austin, a professor at Harvard took a liking to him and encouraged him to take part in George Reisner's archaeological digs in

Egypt and Sudan. The experience of recovering ancient art and relics in the sands of the desert spawned a love and appreciation of art in Austin. After returning from Africa, he went on to improve himself academically and received a degree from Harvard in 1924. Everett went on to become the director of the Wadsworth Athenaeum in Hartford, Connecticut. In this position, he was responsible for acquiring some of the greatest pieces of art in the museum's collection today.

Not only did Austin bring many works by the Old Masters to the museum, but it was also under his direction that some of the earliest American exhibitions of the works of Pablo Picasso and Edward Hopper were organized. Although deeply involved in the art community, Austin began to become more and more interested in the theater. His involvement in the performing arts included magic, and he routinely performed as a magician at the Wadsworth Athenaeum. This interest in the performing arts would not fade during his lifetime.

After his experience with the receptive audience at the Windham Town Hall, Austin made the decision to convert the barn of his house in Windham into a summer theater. When the renovation was complete, the theater had seating for three hundred people, and the stage was more than adequate for the off-Broadway performances that would eventually be shown there. The box seats were brightly enameled sleighs that had been acquired over the years by Austin's mother. Although Austin certainly had the expertise in theatrical performances to make the venture a success, the Windham Playhouse might never have become a reality were it not for the help of the community.

Most notably, Herbert and Rose Crucius were instrumental in the founding of the theater. Herb was given charge of routine maintenance and the stage crews, while his wife directed many of the other activities required to run the operation. Austin frequently even spent time at their home, eating whatever Rose happened to be baking and drinking coffee or eggnog; the eggnog was made by Rose especially for him to help his cough. Certainly many workers of the thirty-five-member crew were locals. Although their job took place behind the curtains, without them the show would have not gone on.

Being a member of the stage crew tasked with preparing the set and scenery would certainly have not been an easy job. Austin was notoriously a stickler for perfection and would not settle for anything less than the best. It is recorded that when a particular scene required a large oak tree, the crew was forced to venture into the nearby woods to locate and cut down the perfect tree. After the tree was felled, it was cut into movable sections and

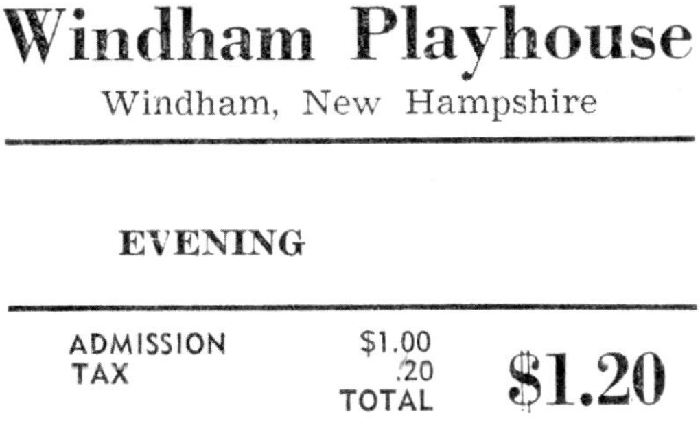
Windham Playhouse
Windham, New Hampshire
EVENING
ADMISSION $1.00
TAX .20
TOTAL $1.20

Left: A 1946 regular admission ticket from the Windham Playhouse. *Author's collection.*

Below: The barn that housed the Windham Playhouse. *Mark Cantrell.*

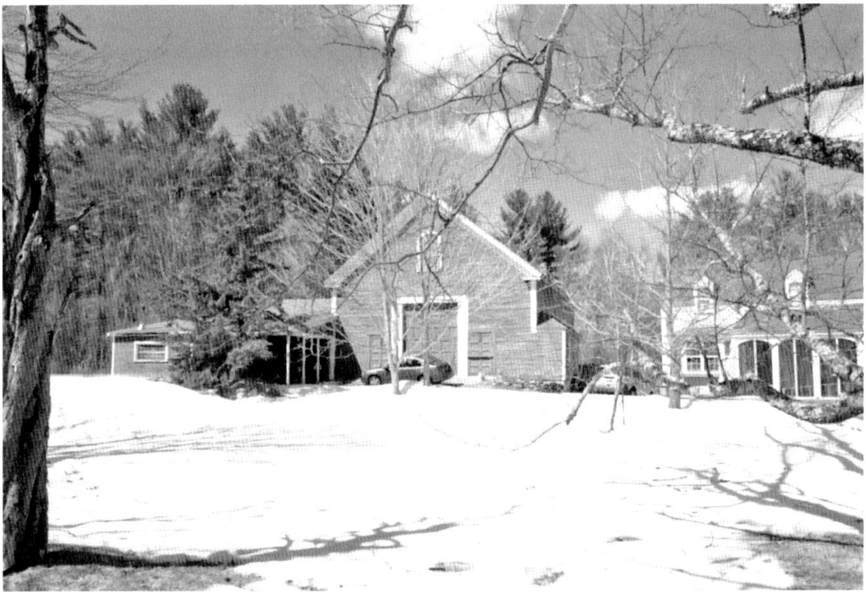

brought into the theater, where it was then reassembled with cables. The finished product was as close to an oak tree as one could have ever wanted.

The detail of the scenery did not end there. It was not unusual for actual staircases and railings to be brought in to perfect the set. Though it would have taken a great deal of time to assemble such detailed sets, Austin did not shy away from designing as many sets as needed for a play. For one play, twelve different sets were constructed, each with its unique challenges for the crew. Some of the sets were nearly thirty-two feet high, and one even had flying scenery.

Such a level of perfection in scenery reflects the quality of shows at Austin's theater. Although many of the shows opened to sellout crowds, the more popular of the shows drew more people than the barn could

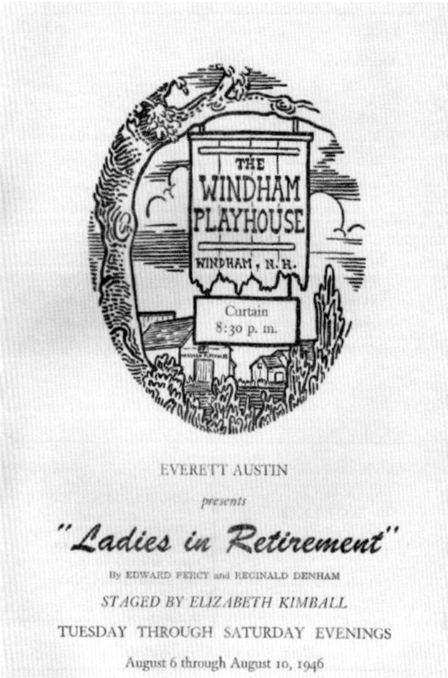

Program for *Ladies in Retirement*, one of the first shows at the Windham Playhouse. *Author's collection.*

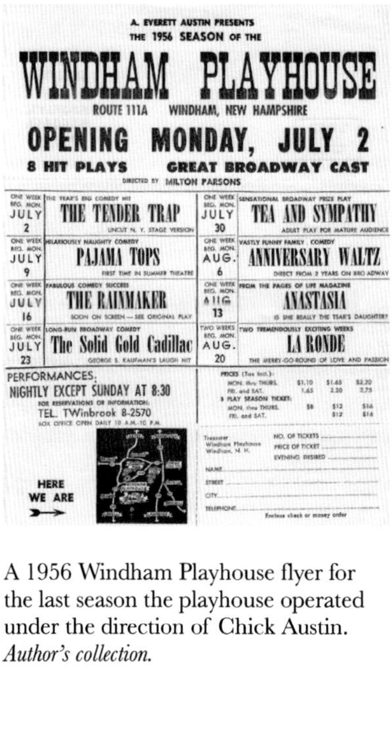

A 1956 Windham Playhouse flyer for the last season the playhouse operated under the direction of Chick Austin. *Author's collection.*

possibly hold; on some nights, as many as one hundred people had to be turned away. The lack of things to do in a small New England town and the quality of the productions made the $1.20 regular admission price a bargain for those interested in the theater or just looking for a couple hours' entertainment. The plays also attracted well-known celebrities, such as Bette Davis, Richard Deacon, Lee Marvin and Rod Steiger. Though the plays themselves would certainly warrant the attendance of well-known performers, some of the stars might have been brought to the Windham Playhouse from the connections Austin had in the theater and art world.

The performers selected by Austin, especially toward the later seasons, were often seasoned professionals who were known to give high-caliber performances. Many of them came from New York, and their transportation, round trip, was provided to them as part of their contract. Housing was also provided to the performers, with three houses and a cottage on Cobbett's Pond being used to accommodate the entire cast. With such amenities included, the fifty-five dollars paid to Lee Marvin for his first performance at the Windham Playhouse would have been quite an attractive offer. There was one drawback for the performers, though: the need and lack of water during the summer months. This problem was only exacerbated by a dry summer.

Therefore, the cabin on the pond, with easy access to the pond for bathing, was always the most popular spot for the cast.

Austin would even join the cast on at least one occasion. In 1956, Austin played Prince Bounine in the play *Anastasia*. As with all the theater's productions, attention to detail was not lacking in any way. Marble fireplaces and French doors were brought in for the scenery, and even antiques and photographs his mother had collected had begun to find their rightful place on the stage.

Shortly before the 1957 season opened, Austin spent his time traveling around the world, an interest he had developed as a child. Spending fall and winter abroad, Austin would return to Windham in the spring to begin to plan the upcoming season. Unfortunately, Austin was plagued by poor health for several seasons into his performances at the theater. Rather than travel the world, he made the decision to spend the winter in France while dedicating the rest of his time to Windham. Located near Austin's theater and home was a cemetery, to which he gave a portion of his adjacent land in the summer of 1956, being sure to reserve a plot for himself, his wife and his children. He had also sketched Egyptian obelisks he intended to

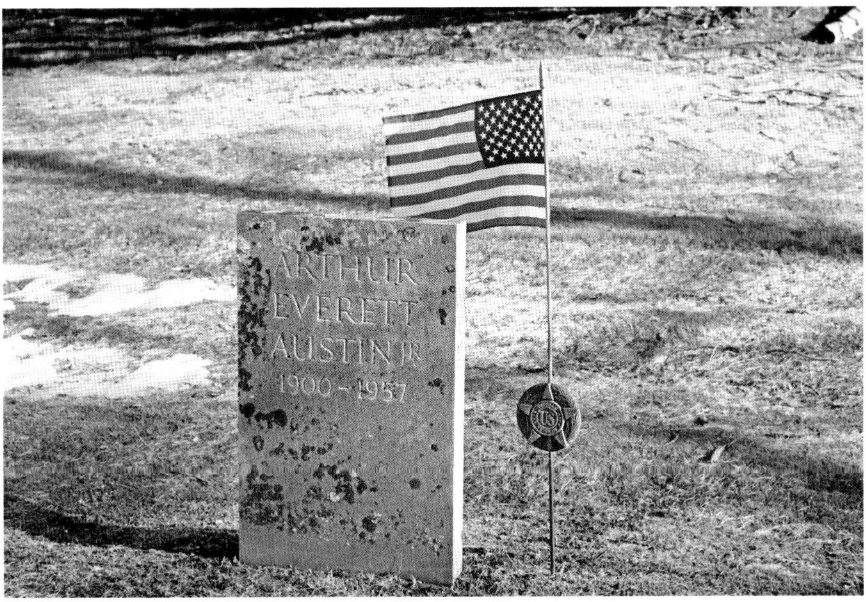

Chick Austin's tombstone in Windham. The plain stone is very different from the obelisk-shaped stone Austin had designed for himself. *Mark Cantrell.*

use as monuments for his family, perhaps a nod toward his days spent on archaeological digs in that country.

Not too much time was spent planning the future burial arrangements, as in March 1957, "Chick" Austin passed away at the age of fifty-six. Prior to his passing, Austin had been adamant about not having or wanting a will. When pressed with questions over his estate, he responded by saying it would have to be fought over. David Garmel took over as director of the Windham Playhouse for the 1957 season, but the settling of Austin's estate necessitated the closing of the theater so the property could be sold. After an eleven-year run, the curtains at the Windham Playhouse closed for the last time.

Austin's funeral was held on the first of April in Hartford, Connecticut. The following day, Austin's body was brought back to Windham to be buried. The ceremony was small relative to the funeral, with only his immediate family and a few friends in attendance. As he had wished, Austin was buried on the plot of land he had reserved for himself and his family, his grave being dug by Herb Crucius. After the casket was lowered into the ground and the grave was filled in, a polished headstone of gray granite was placed at the site, instead of the obelisk Austin had wanted. When it was time to secure the stone to the cement foundation, Crucius struggled with the task, eventually using theatrical screws from the theater to ensure the stone would be a permanent fixture.

18

GREETINGS FROM WINDHAM

Until the advent of social media and smartphones, postcards were the preferred way to send greetings to others. Postcards offered a convenient way for vacationers to show their friends and families what it was like where they were. Although private mailing cards were first introduced around 1898, it was not until several years later that illustrated, hand-colored views became commonplace. However, until 1907, senders were not allowed to write personal messages on the reverse of the postcards; the back was reserved solely for the address. If senders wanted to write about how they were doing or send some other sentiment, they would have been forced to write over the image on the front of the postcard. This problem was solved in 1907, when divided-back postcards were allowed by the postal service. These new postcards devoted half the space on the back for personal messages, with the other half being used for the address. Another major advance in postcard technology came about the same time as the divided-back cards. Real photo postcards allowed any image to be made into a postcard. Rather than send a mass-produced, impersonal postcard, you could send an image of yourself on vacation or a specific view of whatever scene caught their eye.

The postcard industry in Windham started when summer boarders wanted to show their friends and family where they were staying. What better way to do this than a hand-colored postcard view of the home they were staying in? For several cents, you could purchase such a postcard or a postcard showing another scene in town. The proprietors of the

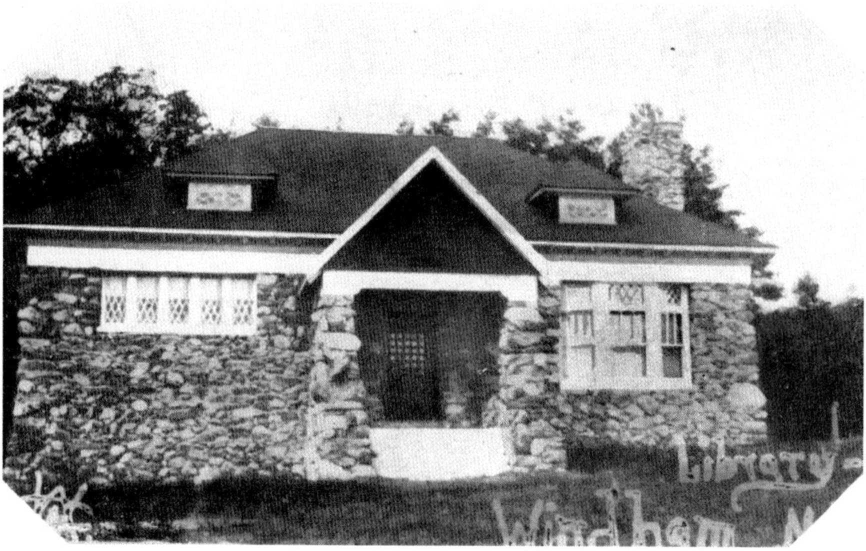

One of the many postcards produced by E.W. Armstrong in the first quarter of the twentieth century. *Author's collection.*

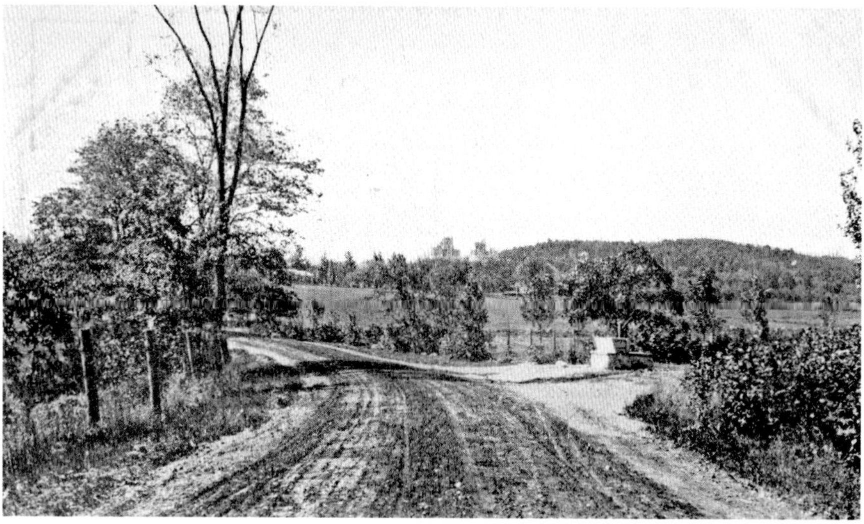

A postcard published by the wife of George W. Johnson that depicts a quaint scene along a road in Windham. *Author's collection.*

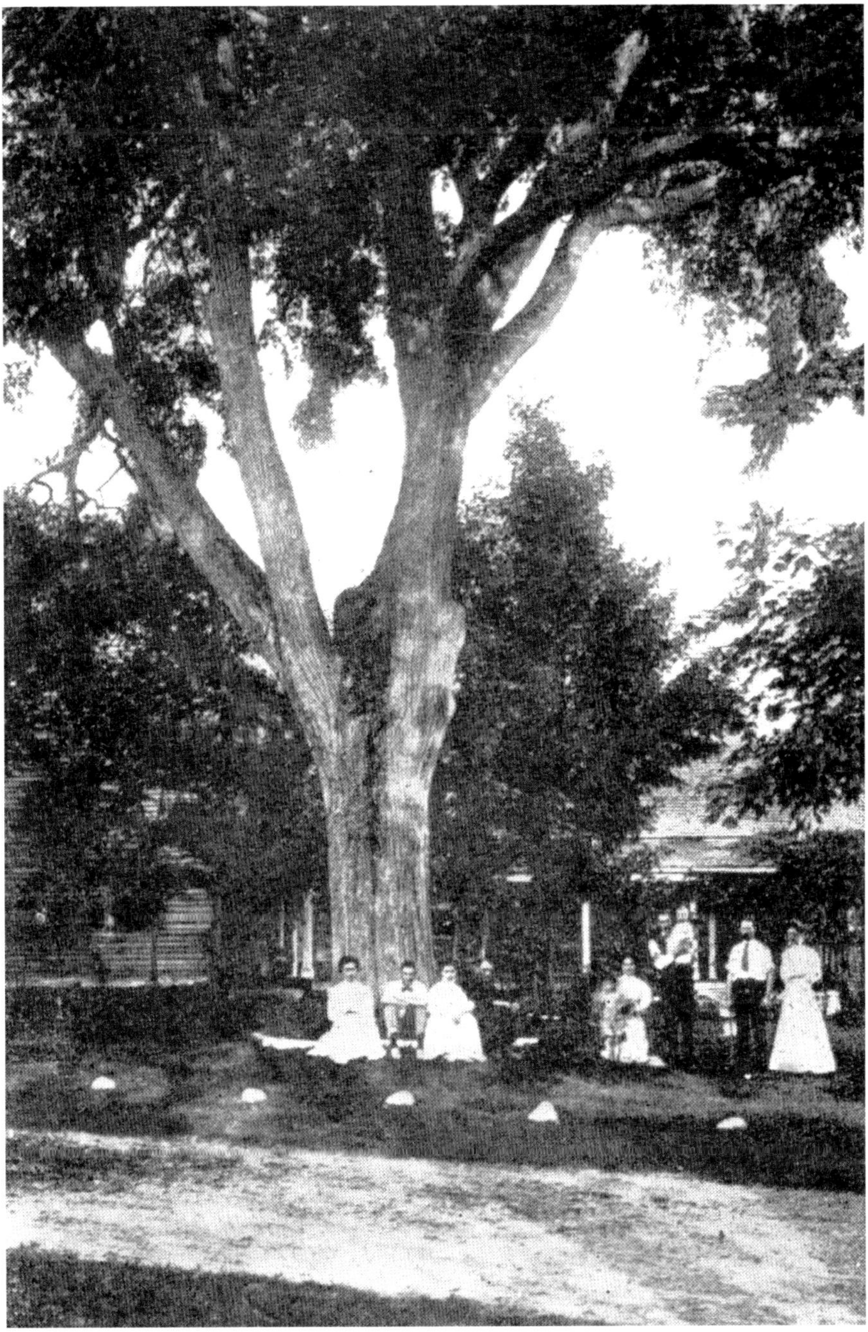

A postcard published by Mrs. M.L. Jackson that shows a group of summer boarders at Elm Farm. *Author's collection.*

boardinghouse would often publish their own cards, usually through Frank W. Swallow, one of the largest postcard publishers in New Hampshire. The wives of George Johnson and George Jackson were among the operators of the town's most popular boardinghouses to publish postcards. Not only was this a great way to supplement the income paid for room and board, but these postcards were also excellent advertising.

In the first quarter of the twentieth century, many vacationers would have been forced to rely on word of mouth in order to choose the best place to stay. Even with an occasional newspaper ad, there would have been no way for a prospective boarder to get some idea of what the building and surroundings looked like. Postcards offered the Jacksons, and other boardinghouse owners, a cheap, efficient way to show anyone anywhere in the nation what their home looked like. A particularly charming postcard of an antique home might have enticed the recipient to spend a few summer days in Windham at the home. Postcards also helped to show outsiders the landscape of Windham.

Not only were postcards available at the individual boardinghouses, but they were also available at general stores. Nathaniel Garland published many views of scenes from various areas of Windham. These were offered for sale in his store at Windham Centre. Whether out of pride, desire for advertising or a combination of both, Garland even published a view of his own store. George Seavey, who operated a mill at the Windham Junction, also published postcards. One of the most popular views he published was of Butterfield's Boulder; the popular attraction certainly warranted the publishing of several different postcards with its image. As many tend to slightly exaggerate when sharing interesting anecdotes with others, it would have been helpful to have the postcard view of Butterfield's Boulder to prove how massive it was; it is doubtful many would have believed it otherwise.

There were countless postcards produced depicting Cobbett's Pond. As the biggest attraction in Windham, it would not be a stretch to say almost every angle of the pond has been captured by a postcard. Beginning just after the turn of the twentieth century, postcard publishers found the pond to be a popular view. The earliest postcards of the pond did not show much more than open land and forested shorelines, with a scarce summer cottage being visible every so often. Mrs. E.G. Rothera, whose family owned a farm near the shore of the pond, was one of the publishers of postcards depicting the pond. However, when public beaches began to open decades later, a new view of the pond became popular. Postcards began to show swimmers diving from a raft or relaxing at the beach. Such postcards could be brought home

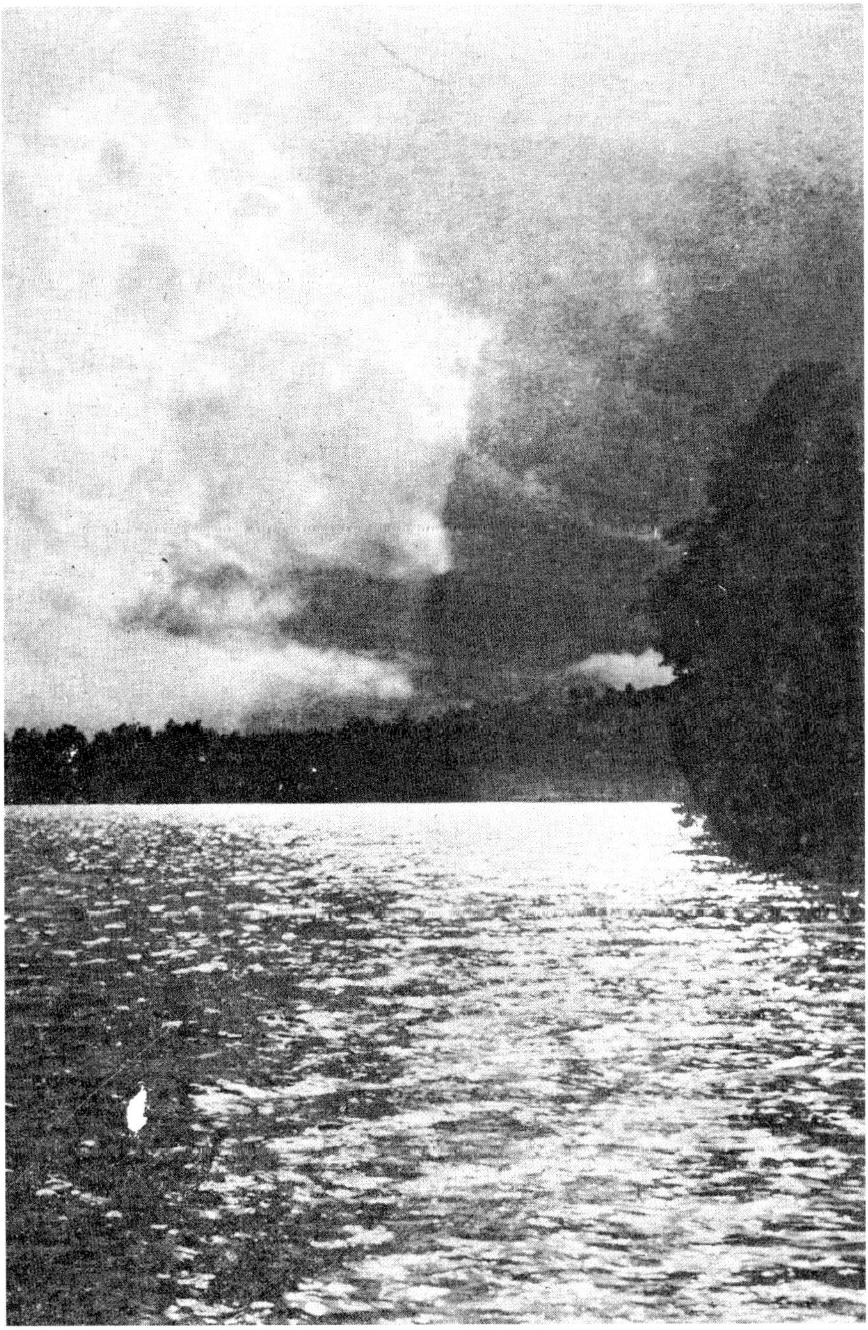

A circa 1910 postcard of an evening sunset on Cobbett's Pond published by Mrs. E.G. Rothera. *Author's collection.*

to be saved as memories of a summer day well spent or sent to show others how much fun could be had at the beach.

As vacation travel to Windham began to decline around the third quarter of the twentieth century, so did the production of Windham postcards. Advances in camera technology allowed anyone an affordable, convenient way to take and develop their own photographs, leaving little reason to purchase postcards. Postcard production, for all intents and purposes, ceased with the closing of the public beaches in the 1970s. Fortunately for future generations, the postcards produced of Windham for approximately seven decades have proven to be a valuable look at Windham's past. The hundreds of unique postcards produced depicting scenes from every part of town represent much more than their original ephemeral purpose.

19

ROBBERY!

Olin J. Cochran was a popular man in Windham, noted for many "firsts" in town as Windham began to emerge into the modern era in the first half of the twentieth century. First, he is recorded as having been one of the first farmers in town to purchase a motorized tractor. He was also one of the first poultry breeders in Windham in the early 1920s. When electricity arrived in town, there was not a single electrician, so Cochran, feeling he could fulfill a public need, became the town's first resident electrician. Cochran also served as town clerk in the 1950s, operating his office out of his home.

It was an ordinary day as Cochran followed his usual routine on the night of Thursday, March 10, 1955. As it was not unusual for people to drop in looking for a license or permit of some kind, Cochran thought nothing of it when two men entered looking to register an automobile. Upon entering the office, one of the men quickly drew a pistol, holding Cochran and his wife at gunpoint. Looking for anything of value they could find in the office, the pair discovered a cashbox containing approximately $112 in cash. The two had clearly taken time to carefully plan the robbery, ripping out the phone line and warning the couple to not attempt alerting anyone.

Being satisfied that they had left nothing of value behind, the pair rushed to an awaiting car driven by an accomplice. However, Cochran did not heed their warning to stay in the office; instead, he grabbed his own .32-caliber pistol and ran after the men. He shot at the fleeing men several times, his shots being answered by a volley of bullets from the robbers. As the exchange of gunfire took place outside the Lowell Road home, Mrs. Cochran ran upstairs where a telephone was located to alert the police. The local and state police were alerted, and roadblocks were quickly set up along all main roads around the scene of the crime.

Although Cochran was physically unscathed from the incident, it was later noticed that a bullet had struck the door jamb of his home—a very close call for the courageous Cochran. The robbers were not so lucky. One was struck twice by Cochran's gunfire. As the Cochrans awaited the arrival of the police to question them about the incident, they tried to recall the details of the men as accurately as they could. When the police began their investigation, it was discovered that the Cochrans had previously had an encounter with one of the robbers. Mrs. Cochran, who was a justice of the peace, performed a marriage ceremony between one of the gun-toting duo and a woman from Windham about six years before.

As the men were armed and very willing to use deadly force, every possible precaution was taken in an attempt to apprehend the men and their getaway driver. Police officials all over New England were alerted to the particulars of the holdup, as well as a description of the getaway car and the two fugitives, as described by the Cochrans. With the Massachusetts border being so close to the scene of the robbery, police from the nearby Massachusetts towns were on especially high alert.

The next day, the men were found by Lawrence, Massachusetts police in a hotel in that city, having checked in under the name of Roy Blake, the same alias that was used when pretending to register an automobile with Cochran. The Lawrence police brought the men to Windham for questioning by Chief Willis Low. When they were questioned separately, the men each declared they were innocent and denied any knowledge of the robbery. However, when they were brought in together for questioning, the three men confessed to the hold up and gave police an accurate account of the roles each had played.

As one of the men, identified as Robert G. Scully, was suffering from two bullet wounds, he was brought to Lawrence General Hospital, where he remained under police guard. At the hospital, doctors removed a bullet from just beneath his left shoulder blade, as well as another one lodged in his upper left arm. Scully was further identified as being twenty-eight years old and from Salem, New Hampshire. J. Casey, a twenty-six-year-old man also from Salem, and Frederick M. Cole, twenty-five years old, of Derry, were also taken into custody during the hotel room raid; Cole was the suspected getaway driver.

As it came time for Scully to be released from the hospital and sent to the Hillsborough County Jail, there was some suspicion that he may also have perpetrated the recent robbery of the Civic Theatre in Portsmouth, New Hampshire. The theater cashier, Alberta Maddix, was called on by the police to make a preliminary identification of Scully. If she answered affirmatively that he matched the description of the man who held her up, then she was to be brought to Manchester, New Hampshire, to aid in establishing proof of his guilt.

However, Maddix was unable to positively identify Scully as the man who held up her theater at gunpoint, getting away with seventy dollars. In fact, Maddix found no resemblance between Scully and the real bandit. Unfortunately for the local police, they were not given the quick resolution to the case they had hoped for.

When the trio appeared in court on March 22, they all pleaded innocent and wanted their cases to be heard by a jury. Scully and Casey were charged with armed robbery, while Cole was charged with accessory to armed robbery. Judge Dennis E. Sullivan ordered each man held on $5,000 bail; otherwise, they would await trial in the Hillsborough County Jail.

On March 30, Frederick Cole was sentenced to four to seven years in the New Hampshire State Prison after being convicted of being an accessory to armed robbery. Even though he had previously pleaded not guilty, when he realized the evidence was overwhelmingly against him, he entered a guilty plea in the Hillsborough County Superior Court. It would be another four weeks before Scully and Jones were tried and sentenced on April 28. On that day, Scully and Jones both also decided against making a case for their innocence, entering guilty pleas before Judge John H. Leahy. Both were sentenced to six to ten years in the New Hampshire State Prison after being convicted of armed robbery.

It did not take long after the incident for the Cochrans to return to their usual routines at their home office, which also served as the center of their real estate and insurance business. Twenty-one years after the robbery, Cochran died at the age of eighty at the Alexander Eastman Hospital in Derry following an illness.

20
HOW WINDHAM HAS CELEBRATED ITS HISTORY

Throughout the history of America, towns and cities across the nation have had the occasion to celebrate their anniversaries. Such occasions give each generation of residents an opportunity to show pride in their town's unique history. These celebrations help to preserve history by stirring up interest in the past, as well as getting residents directly involved in the town's history. Windham has benefitted from several of these historic celebrations throughout its nearly three-hundred-year history. Anniversaries of Nutfield have also been an important part of the celebration of Windham, as Nutfield represents the earliest part of the town's history.

Nutfield's 150th Anniversary: 1869

Windham as a town had no official part in the June 10, 1869 celebration of Nutfield's 150th anniversary. In March 1868, the selectmen of Derry formed a committee to work with Londonderry for the purpose of celebrating the anniversary of Nutfield for the first time in its history. No significant progress was made toward planning the event until Londonderry appointed a committee to work on behalf of the town in November 1868. As parts of Manchester were originally a part of Nutfield, that city also formed a committee to work with the two other towns. However, Manchester did not take a significant part in the planning of the 1869 event.

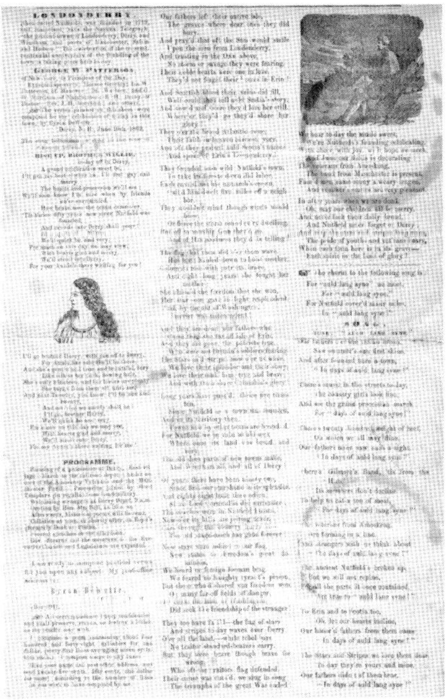

An 1869 broadside printed for the celebration of the 150th anniversary of the settlement of Nutfield. *Author's collection.*

The first meeting of the committees of Londonderry and Derry took place on December 9, 1868. At this meeting, a committee was formed with members of each town's committees. This arrangement allowed the new committee to work on the major planning while each town's individual committees could focus on the more detailed tasks at hand. George F. Adams of Derry was appointed as the group's chairman. The other two appointed positions of secretary and treasurer were filled by Robert Mack and Jonathan McAllister, respectively; both men were from Londonderry. Although Windham as a town did not participate in the planning, two of Windham's prominent citizens were chosen as members of the committee. Deacon Samuel Campbell and George Weston were the two men chosen to take part in the celebration.

At one of the subsequent meetings of the committee, the date of June 10 was selected for the celebration, despite the first settlers arriving in Nutfield on April 22. As the event needed to be easily accessible to the townspeople of all three towns, Derry Depot was chosen as the location. The particulars of the event were established over the next several months, including arrangements for notable speakers. As the day of the first celebration of Nutfield neared, the residents of Windham eagerly anticipated one of the first major celebrations of the town's earliest settlement. Prior to 1869, there were only a few significant celebrations in town, including a major celebration of the Fourth of July about forty years prior.

When June 10 finally arrived, people came from Londonderry, Derry and Windham, as well as the surrounding localities, to take part in the once-in-a-lifetime event. Those residing near Derry Depot started their day with the ringing of the church bell and the ceremonial firing of a cannon. Shortly after 8:00 a.m., a procession formed in the Upper Village of Derry. The procession was led by Henry E. Eastman in the capacity of chief marshal. Eastman led the Amoskeag Veterans and the Manchester Cornet Band as they followed their short route around Derry. First making its way through the village, the group then continued on to the Adams Female Academy and then back to its starting point. From there, the procession continued on to the Lower Village of Derry, where a large tent had been erected for the occasion on "Doak's Plains." It was here that students from Pinkerton Academy joined the group, having been led there by a Mr. Hazen. Many of the pupils from Derry's other schools were also marshalled to the plains by Hazen.

At 10:00 a.m., a train arrived from Boston, which had picked up many passengers from Londonderry, Windham and Salem along its way to Derry. Prominent citizens from Boston, Lowell and some of the surrounding locales also arrived at the Derry Depot by train. At this point, the crowds grew even larger, having been joined by the members of Londonderry's Good Templar, who were dressed in their full regalia. At last, the entire crowd for the day had formed, and it would not be long before the day's events began.

The first event of the day was an oration by Charles H. Bell, who later became the governor of New Hampshire, which took place at 11:00 a.m. This was followed by the recitation of historical poems. One such poem was written by Byron DeWolfe of Nashua for the event. It recounts, in the form of a poem, the settlement of Nutfield, as well as historical events that had taken place since the founding. In only one stanza is there a mention of Windham:

Long years have passed, thrice five times ten,
Since Nutfield as a town was founded,
And in its territory then,
Towns now by other towns are bounded;
For Nutfield we in vain would seek,
Where once its land was broad and very,
The old does parts of new towns make,
And Windham all, and all of Derry!

At about noon, once all the poems had been read, the attendees reconvened as a group on Doak's Plains, which was located to the east of Derry Depot. This gave the crowds an opportunity to attend to any urgent business or obtain much-needed refreshments. The remainder of the orations of the day were made following this short interlude.

George W. Patterson, the former lieutenant governor of New York, was chosen to preside over the event as president. Patterson was raised in Londonderry and attended Pinkerton Academy. Thus, his political prominence and Nutfield roots made him an excellent choice to give one of the day's most anticipated addresses. Horace Greeley, the much-noted editor of the *New York Tribune*, also gave a speech that day. Other speakers at the event included E.H. Derby of Boston and Samuel H. Taylor of Phillips Academy in Andover. The end of the speeches signaled the end of the event, and the Windham residents in attendance returned home with many memories of the day. It was recorded by Leonard A. Morrison that the events of June 10 "would never be forgotten by those present."

Windham's 150th Anniversary: 1892

Prior to 1892, Windham had never celebrated the anniversary of its township. The need for such a celebration was recognized as Leonard Morrison began working on his history of Windham in the early 1880s. It was at that time that some of the descendants of the early settlers and founders of the town proposed that there be a celebration for the 150th anniversary. However, it was not until about 1891 that much of the detailed planning was completed for the event.

Although Windham was incorporated on February 23, the winter months would certainly not have been conducive for an outdoor celebration. June was chosen not for any particular significance but rather for its promise of many warm, summer days. Before the details of the event were planned, it was necessary to prepare a petition for the town selectmen to hold a special meeting for the purpose of planning an official day to observe the anniversary. The ease of obtaining the signatures of residents on the petition reflected the excitement throughout town for the impending celebration.

A committee was chosen to oversee the planning of the event at a town hall meeting on January 23, 1892. After it was unanimously voted that there would be a celebration of the anniversary, two members from each of the seven school districts were chosen to become members on the committee. The first task of the committee was to raise the funds for the June celebration. After just a couple weeks of brainstorming, the idea of holding a C-themed supper was chosen as the best option for fundraising. Only foods that began with the letter *c* were served at the supper, which took place in the town hall.

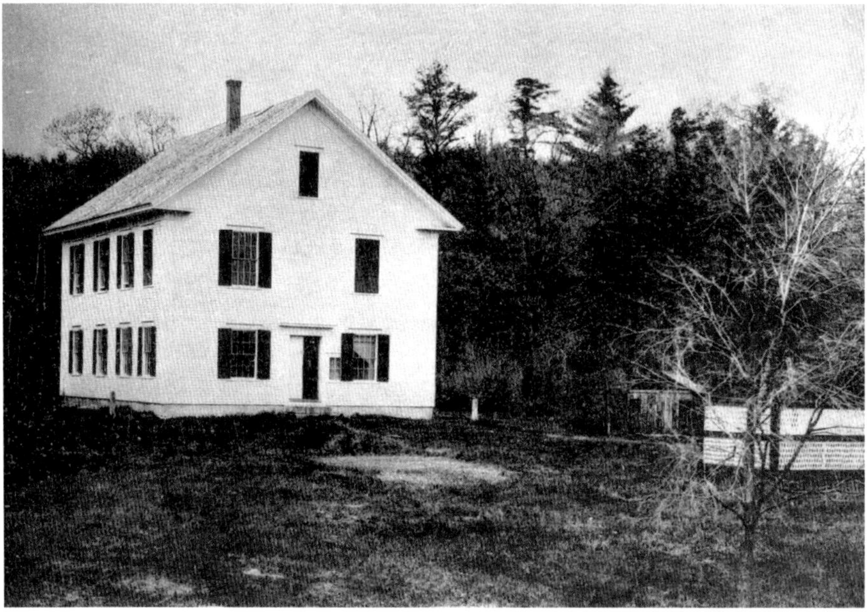

The town hall as it would have appeared during the 1892 celebration. *From* History of Windham in New Hampshire (Rockingham County), 1719–1883.

Some of the foods included clam chowder, chicken pie, Chinese tea, cream pie and chocolate pudding.

Richard Carle, who later became a well-known film actor in the first half of the twentieth century, was hired to provide comedic entertainment for the night. Carle's performance was included in the price of admission for the meal: forty cents for adults and twenty cents for children under the age of twelve. In order to supplement the income from ticket sales, ice cream and flowers were also sold at the supper.

There was an excellent turnout for the event, and $115 was raised between ticket sales and other purchases. As a foot and a half of snow had fallen by the morning of the twelfth, and the winds were particularly strong that day, the success of the event serves as a testament to the townspeople's enthusiasm for the event and for the summer celebration it would pay for. The following day, an executive committee was formed for planning the celebration of the anniversary, and several subcommittees were established. Over the next month, one of the most important tasks of the executive committee was to select the proper place to hold the event. Abel Dow, owner of the Granite State Grove, offered the town use of the entire park, save the skating rink. However, the town declined, and the town center was chosen instead.

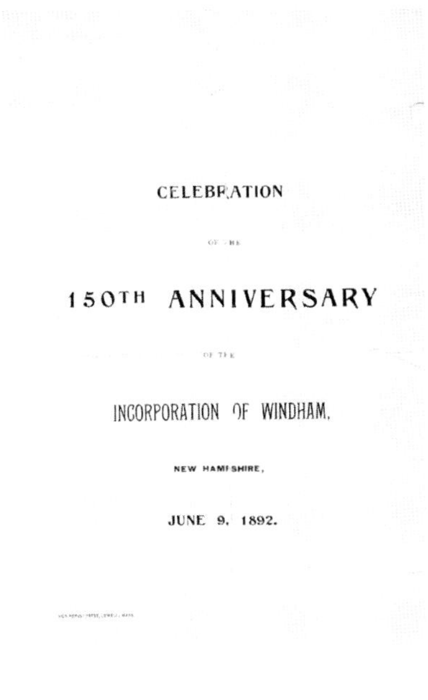

The cover of a program produced for the celebration of the 150th anniversary of the incorporation of Windham in 1892. *Author's collection.*

After several more months of planning, the fateful day had finally arrived. The day commenced with the ringing of the bell at the Presbyterian Church at sunrise. Around 9:30 a.m. John H. Dinsmoor arrived with the Haverhill Band at Schoolhouse No. 6, where the pupils of that district joined the procession as it made its way to the town hall. When the procession reached the town hall, its members were greeted by the crowds who had been waiting in anticipation for the commencement of the events of the day. Reverend Blanchard of Andover, Massachusetts, opened the ceremony by reading from the scriptures, which was followed by a prayer led by Reverend Berry of Pelham, New Hampshire.

Following a short performance by the Windham Glee Club, Leonard Morrison took the stage and delivered his welcoming address. This was received well by the crowd, but many of the younger people in the crowd likely hoped for a rather terse speech, as it was to be followed by a more lively performance by the Haverhill Band. After a short but dynamic performance by the band, the crowd was treated to a reading of the original petition asking for a town charter, the document responsible for the incorporation of Windham as a town separate from Londonderry. It was as a result of this petition that the day's celebration was taking place. The town clerk John Cochran was selected to read the petition.

Before another interlude of music by the band, Morrison recited a poem that was written by Margaret Dinsmoor especially for the event. The poem captured the story of the early Scotch-Irish settlers who first settled Nutfield. James Dinsmoor of Sterling, Illinois, followed the performance of the band, delivering the historical address. He was invited on behalf of the executive committee in order to give the address. Keeping with the theme of interjecting music between the readings and speeches, the Windham Glee Club performed again, this time performing the song "The Rock of Liberty." The group received a roaring round of applause for its rendition.

When Morrison took the stage again to address the crowds, he realized that the time had passed much faster than he had originally planned. There would not be time for a letter mailed via ship from Londonderry, Ireland, which was written by Reverend Gilbert Alexander Kennedy to be read at Windham's anniversary. Instead, there would be an intermission during which the day's dinner would be held. Once Morrison departed from the stage, he joined 139 speakers and distinguished guests on the first floor of the town hall, where five long tables were set up. The schoolteachers, pupils and other town officials, which in total numbered about 100, ate their dinners across the street in the Bartley house.

The remainder of the crowd amounted to about 1,500 people, all of whom were served their dinners in a large tent that had been erected at the town center. After everyone was seated in the tent, waiters began to bustle about their respective sections, serving 1,500 packages of previously prepared food. Although the meal was not as elaborate as that being enjoyed by the distinguished guests, it still satisfied the many people in attendance. Each person was given meat, cake or bread and a banana, which Morrison noted as being separated from the rest of the food by a "Japanese napkin." Coffee was served with the meal, having been brewed in Boston and then shipped in large tanks to Windham. The coffee, as well as cold water, was available to all the guests of the celebration.

Just before 3:00 p.m., the crowds gathered again, and Morrison took to the stage to give a short toast to the town before the next address was given. Those not wishing to remain at the event had the opportunity to leave by train for Lawrence and Boston at Windham Junction. Many in the crowd who remained at the celebration listened attentively to the several speeches that followed, mostly on subjects concerning Windham. William H. Anderson delivered a speech on the history of Nutfield. Between every three or four speeches, the band played, giving the audience a most welcome intermission from the orations.

Albert Pillsbury's speech concluded the orations of the day, and this was followed by a rendition of "America" sung by the audience, with music provided by the band. After the audience had finished its joyous performance, Morrison delivered the closing address, and then the band played for the last time that day, signaling the end of the first celebration of Windham's incorporation. Large wagons then arrived at the town center to bring those traveling home by train to Windham Junction. Those who resided in town returned home with the knowledge that months of hard work and planning had paid off.

NUTFIELD'S 200TH ANNIVERSARY: 1919

The 200th anniversary of Nutfield was the most momentous celebration that has taken place in the town's almost three-hundred-year history. All three towns had grown significantly since the last anniversary in 1869, resulting in much larger crowds for the event. While the previous Nutfield celebration was limited to a single day, the 200th anniversary was celebrated over the course of three days, August 24, 25 and 26. The size of the event required over a dozen committees and hundreds of people to plan each part. The committees were responsible for the gamut of duties, including arranging transportation, creating the souvenir program and organizing the pageant. One of the committees was also tasked with identifying historic spots in what was Nutfield, which helped to generate greater interest in these sites throughout the community. Although the majority of the sites that were published by the committee were located in Derry, there were several in Windham, one of which was the site of the first settlement on Copp's Hill near Cobbett's Pond. The site of John Gregg's death at the hands of Indians in 1721, as well as Indian Rock, was also included.

In the days leading up to the celebration, many local businesses took advantage of the excitement to use Nutfield for promotional purposes. Dudley's Jewelry Store in Derry showcased a drum from 1720 that belonged to pioneering settler James Gregg; it had been exhibited for the 150th anniversary, as well. Also, a gun that was owned by Robert "Rustic Bard" Dinsmoor was on display in the window of the store. Both of these items of great historical significance were on loan to Dudley by H.P. Dinsmoor.

Although the event was primarily attended by residents of Londonderry, Derry and Windham, some individuals with ancestral connections to one of the Nutfield towns made trips of hundreds of miles to take part in the celebration. Reverend A.B. Cristy, whose ancestors lived in Windham, traveled approximately 650 miles from Panesville, Ohio, to spend the week of the Nutfield celebration in Derry. As the celebration was held in Derry, the only chance Cristy would have had to participate in an event in Windham would have been the Windham Women's Club dance in honor of Nutfield on the previous Saturday.

The celebration began on August 24, a Sunday, at the historic First Church in East Derry. It was here that Alan B. Shepard, the father of the astronaut with the same name, played the organ music, which opened the exercises of the day. This was followed by readings from the scriptures, recitation of hymns and the Schubert Quartette's singing several songs. Several of the

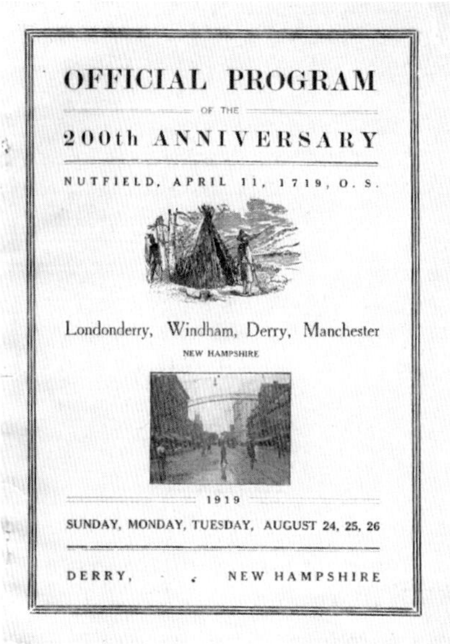

A 1919 official souvenir program produced for the 200th anniversary of Nutfield. *Author's collection.*

other churches around Derry also held services that day, some of which honored the anniversary of Nutfield. Only ecclesiastical services were held that day; the other events were to take place on the following two days.

The festivities on Monday began at 8:00 a.m. with a parade of "antiques and horribles," with prizes given in several categories. The top prize awarded was twenty-five dollars for the "most horrible band," with the stipulation that in order to win the prize, the band had to be no fewer than nine pieces. Aside from the category for the most horrible parade float, the other prizes were awarded in several costume categories. A panel of five judges was organized to pick the winners in each category.

At the conclusion of the parade, much of the crowd made its way to the baseball field where the Salem Cadet Band performed a concert prior to the baseball game. At 10:00 a.m. sharp, fans of baseball, young and old, remained at the field to watch the first game of that day's doubleheader between two rivals, the Derry Athletic Association and McElwain of Manchester. Those who were not interested in baseball or did not have the patience to sit through every inning had the opportunity to watch a whippet race take place on Birch Street. For those not familiar with whippet racing, whippets are medium-sized dog breeds, often described as smaller greyhounds.

The baseball game ended just before noon, giving the spectators and players an opportunity to watch a once-in-a-lifetime stunt. "Daredevil Smith" of Newburyport, Massachusetts, ascended in a hot air balloon, from which he leapt with only a parachute after reaching the desired height. What a sight! Such a stunt would have been almost unheard of in southern New Hampshire. Unlike today, parachute technology was primitive, and only trained stuntmen undertook such endeavors.

This exhilarating event was followed by a parade that was led by mounted police from Derry. Following the officers were eight divisions of several different groups, the first of which was led by Alan B. Shepard. Each division included a band, as well as a variety of veterans and fraternal groups. The fire department, as well as many local businesses, also took part in the parade. H.P. Hood & Sons, was a featured part of the fourth division. Hood was the largest local dairy operation and obtained a portion of its milk from Windham farms.

At 3:00 p.m., the second baseball game of the day began, giving the team that lost the first game a chance to tie the day's score with a win. While the fans were cheering on their hometown team, a bicycle race was held nearby, with prizes awarded for the first three finishers. The young man who finished first was awarded a loving cup worth $15.00, a prize that he could proudly display for years to come. Finishing in second place was worthy of a $2.50 gold piece, which could have been spent eagerly at the day's festivities or saved for a rainy day. A much more practical prize was given to the third place finisher: a brand-new bicycle lamp for early morning and evening riding.

With America's newfound love of all things flying since the Wright brothers' first flight, it was fitting that there was an airplane demonstration at the celebration. George Watkins of the Downing Aerial Transportation Company flew an airplane over Derry to the delight of the crowds. This was followed a couple hours later by another hot air balloon ascension, but this time, there was no daredevil to jump out.

The day's events ended with a pageant held on the grounds of Pinkerton Academy. The pageant was written to showcase the common history of Londonderry, Derry and Windham. This included a reenactment of the settlement of Nutfield until its incorporation as Londonderry. The pageant then continued on with various scenes from the French and Indian War, a typical colonial wedding, as well as the advent of modern industry. One thousand seats were made available for the pageant, which gives an idea of how popular the event was expected to be. There were likely some Windham residents who traveled to Derry to purchase their tickets at Warren's News Store or Stockdale's; each ticket was sold for one quarter. For the few in Windham who might have desired to drive by automobile to Pinkerton, they could enjoy the pageant with the assurance that their vehicles would be under police protection for the entirety of the event. For the rest, trains arrived and left Derry every ten minutes for an hour or so before and after the event.

With the busiest day of the Nutfield celebration over, there were only a few events scheduled for Tuesday, and none like the stunts and sporting events of the previous day. At 10:00 a.m., Reverend Jesse G. MacMurphy gave his historical address, which was then followed by other various addresses. When the speeches concluded a few hours later, a banquet was held in Adams Memorial Hall for the celebration's presidents, as well as special guests and their wives. However, it was also possible for others to attend the banquet with the purchase of a $1.75 ticket.

Those who could not justify spending that much on a ticket or just had little interest in attending the banquet had the opportunity to witness a most unusual gathering. At 1:30 p.m., a reunion was held for those who had attended the previous Nutfield anniversary in 1869. As it had been fifty years earlier, it was unlikely that there were many members of the original group in attendance. When one thinks about all the changes and history that took place within that half century, it is astounding to imagine what those who were part of the reunion witnessed. It is unknown if any of the Windham residents who attended the 1869 reunion were part of the reunion.

Half an hour later, the final addresses of the celebration of the 200th anniversary of Nutfield began, lasting for a couple hours. When the last word of the last address was spoken, there was only one activity left for this historic event. A firework demonstration was set to take place at 8:30 p.m., and crowds gathered on the field of the Derry Athletic Association to watch the sky light up in various colors as the 200th anniversary of the settlement of Nutfield came to a conclusion, with the next major anniversary half a century away.

BIBLIOGRAPHY

"Along Quiet Shores: A Sketch of Cobbett's Pond." *Granite Monthly*, April 1898.

Boda, Rose, et al. *Rural Oasis: History of Windham, New Hampshire, 1883–1975*. Canaan, CT: Phoenix Publishing Company, 1975.

Buxton, Andrew. *Cash Carriers in Shops*. Oxford, UK: Shire, 2008.

Chapman, George T. *Sketches of the Alumni of Dartmouth College: From the First Graduation in 1771 to the Present Time; with a Brief History of the Institution.* Cambridge, MA: Riverside Press, 1867.

Derry Enterprise. "News and Notes." August 26, 1919.

Derry News. "At Canobie." August 30, 1901.

———. January 13, 1882.

Evening Star. "Races at Aqueduct." April 22, 1904.

Flinton, Sister Martina. *The Searles Saga*. N.p.: self-published, 1976.

Gaddis, Eugene R. *Magician of the Modern: Chick Austin and the Transformation of the Arts in America*. New York: Alfred Knopf, 2000.

"Hugh Duffy." Wikipedia.com. https://en.wikipedia.org/wiki/Hugh_Duffy.

"J. Ernest Hammond." Ancestry.com. http://archiver.rootsweb.ancestry.com/th/read/RIGENWEB/2002-06/1023912826.

"Lambing Time." Henry Sheldon Museum of Vermont History. http://henrysheldonmuseum.org/lambing-time.

Mack, Robert C. *Londonderry Celebration: June 10, 1869*. Manchester, NH: John B. Clarke, 1870.

"Merino: The Silk of Wool." Regency Redingote. https://regencyredingote.wordpress.com/2015/02/06/merino-the-silk-of-wool.

Morrison, Leonard Allison. *History and Proceedings of the Celebration of the One Hundredth and Fiftieth Anniversary of the Incorporation of the Settlement of Windham in New Hampshire, Held June 9, 1892.* Windham, NH: Executive Committee, 1892.

———. *The History of Windham in New Hampshire (Rockingham County), 1719–1883.* Boston: Cupples, Upham & Company, 1883.

Nashua Telegraph. "Olin Cochran." May 29, 1976.

———. "Salem Pair Identified as Men Who Held Up Windham Clerk." March 11, 1955.

———. "Sentenced as Accessory After Windham Hold Up." March 31, 1955.

———. "Three Held in $5,000 Bail for Windham Robbery." March 24, 1955.

———. "Windham Public Beaches, Water Safety Discussed." September 20, 1970.

Pittsburg Dispatch. "We Won in the Wet." June 26, 1889.

Portsmouth Herald. "Confessed Bandit Brought to NH." March 14, 1955.

———. "Largest Free Boulder in NH at Windham." January 25, 1937.

———. "Theater Cashier Fails to Identify Windham Bandit." March 21, 1955.

———. "Trio Held in Bail for Jury Trial in Windham Robbery." March 23, 1955.

———. "Windham Bandits Get 6–10 Year Sentences." April 28, 1955.

Provincial and State Papers. Vol. 13. New Hampshire, 1884.

"Rev. Thomas Cobbet." *Granite Monthly*, January 1917.

Saint Paul Daily Globe. "Cowboys Cinched." July 28, 1888.

———. "They Threw It Away." October 1, 1887.

Souvenir Program Committee. *Official Program of the 200th Anniversary.* Derry, NH: News-Enterprise Press, 1919.

Sun. "Duffy's First Baseball Game." November 6, 1889.

"Wallace Fessenden." Wikipedia.org. https://en.wikipedia.org/wiki/Wallace_Fessenden.

Whittier, John Greenleaf. *The Prose Works of John Greenleaf Whittier in Three Volumes.* Vol. 2. Cambridge, MA: Houghton, Mifflin, and Company, 1892.

"William Jarvis (merchant)." Wikipedia.org. https://en.wikipedia.org/wiki/William_Jarvis_(merchant).

"Windham…Change for Lawrence and Boston!" *B&M Bulletin*, Winter 1976–77.

"The Wreck of the *Snow Catherine*." Accessible Archives Inc., August 3, 2012. http://www.accessible-archives.com/2012/08/the-wreck-of-the-snow-catherine.

ABOUT THE AUTHOR

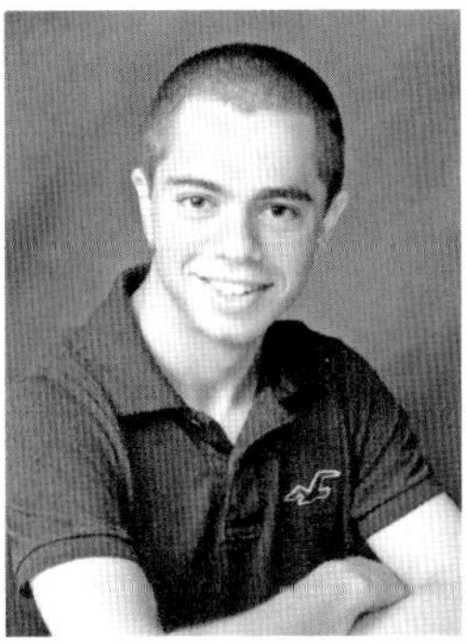

Derek Saffie is a native of Windham, New Hampshire. For the past several years, he has collected numerous relics from Windham's past. He is an alternate member of the Windham Historic Commission and a trustee of the Windham Museum. In addition to serving on both boards, he is a member of the Windham Historical Society. For his work with local history, he has been featured in several newspapers, including the *Lawrence Eagle Tribune* and the *Manchester Union Leader*. Derek is currently pursuing a bachelor's degree in computer science at Merrimack College in North Andover, Massachusetts. His website is www.windhamnhhistory.com.